Arnold Whitaker Oxford

English Cookery Books

to the Year 1850

Arnold Whitaker Oxford

English Cookery Books

to the Year 1850

ISBN/EAN: 9783944350356

Auflage: 1

Erscheinungsjahr: 2013

Erscheinungsort: Bremen, Deutschland

@ Kochbuch-Verlag in Access Verlag GmbH, Fahrenheitstr. 1, 28359 Bremen. Alle Rechte beim Verlag und bei den jeweiligen Lizenzgebern.

ENGLISH COOKERY BOOKS

TO THE YEAR 1850

BY

ARNOLD WHITAKER OXFORD, M.A., M.D.

HENRY FROWDE
OXFORD UNIVERSITY PRESS
LONDON, EDINBURGH, NEW YORK, TORONTO, MELBOURNE
AND BOMBAY
1913

CONTENTS

	PAGE
ENGLISH COOKERY BOOKS, 1500-1850	1
APPENDIX	182
INDEX OF AUTHORS	185
INDEX OF TITLES	188

BIBLIOGRAPHY

1864. Host and Guest, by A. V. Kirwan.
1874. Publishers' Weekly (New York), vol. vi, 388, 421. Two lists by H. W. Hageman.
1875. A Book about the Table, by John Cordy Jeaffreson, vol. 2, chap. 17.
1890. Bibliographie Gastronomique, by Georges Vicaire.
1893. Old Cookery Books, by W. Carew Hazlitt. Second edition.
1895. National Review, vol. 24, 676; 25, 776. Two papers by Col. A. Kenney Herbert.
1902. The Pleasures of the Table, by George H. Ellwanger.
1903. My Cookery Books, by Elizabeth Robins Pennell.
1908. A Book of Simples, by H. W. Lewer.
1909. Notes from a Collector's Catalogue with a bibliography of English cookery books, by A. W. Oxford.

PREFATORY NOTE

In a book called 'Notes from a Collector's Catalogue'[1] I gave a list of English cookery books to the year 1700, with the name of the library in which each could be found and a collation of the various editions. The present list contains the title-pages of English books on cookery and domestic economy to the year 1850.

I may repeat what was said in the former book, that my real interest is not in cookery but in the combination of cookery with medicine, which is found in most of the early books, and which, continuing through the first quarter of the nineteenth century, was gradually destroyed by the growth of railways.

John and Edward Bumpus, 1909.

ENGLISH COOKERY BOOKS

1500 THIS IS THE BOKE OF COKERY
Here beginneth a noble boke of festes royalle and Cokery a boke for a pryncis housholde or any other estates ; and the makynge therof as ye shall fynde more playnly within this boke.

Emprynted without temple barre by Richard Pynson in the yere of our lorde. M D.

This title is given in Ames and Herbert,[1] where it is stated that the Dowager Duchess of Portland brought the book from Bulstrode to London for Herbert to examine.

A book called ' A noble booke of feastes royall, and of Cookerie, for Princes housholde, or any other estate, and the making thereof ', is given by Maunsell[2] as having been printed by John Byddell. This is doubtless the same book, and the date would be between 1533 and 1540.

1508 HERE BEGYNNETH THE BOKE OF KERVYNGE.
This book is in the Cambridge Library. The colophon is 'Here endeth the boke of servyce and kervynge and sewynge and all maner of offyce in his kynde unto a prynce or ony other estate and all the feestes in the yere. Emprynted by Wynkyn de Worde at London in the Fletestrete at the sygne of the sonne. The yere of our lorde, M,CCCCC,VIII.'

The British Museum has a copy with the colophon, ' Here endeth the boke of servyce and kervynge and sewynge and all maner of offyce in his kynde unto a prynce or ony other estate and all the feestes in the yere. Emprynted by Wynkyn de Worde at London in Flete strete at the sygne of the sonne. The yere of our lorde god, M CCCCC XIII.'

Each of the above copies is a small quarto ; A with 6 leaves, B with 6. The book was reprinted by Abraham Veale (i.e.

[1] Typographical Antiquities (1812 edition), ii. 420.
[2] The first part of the Catalogue of English printed Bookes (1595).

between 1558 and 1586) as 'THE BOOKE OF CARVYNG', and twice by E. Allde as 'THE BOOKE OF CARVING AND SEWING', the first edition being without a date, the second dated 1613. These are each 12°; the former A to C in eights, the latter two A to C₄ in eights.

The book was added in 1597 to 'The second part of the Good Hus-wifes Jewell', and in 1631 to John Murrell's 'Two bookes of cookerie and carving'.

The book was edited for the Early English Text Society in 1868 by F. W. Furnivall.

It begins with a list of terms which are to be used by the carver, e.g. Lyft that swanne, unlace that cony, dysplaye that crane, dysfygure that pecocke, untache that curlew, alaye that fesande, wynge that patryche, mynce that plover, and so on.

Later on the duties of the butler are laid down and a list of his wines given, viz. Reed wyne, whyte wyne, clared wyne, osey, capricke, campolet, renysche wyne, malvesey, bastarde, tyet, romney, muscadell, clarrey, raspys, vernage wyne, cut, pymente, and ypocras.

The chamberlain's duties are strange. 'The chaumberlayne must be dylygent & clenly in his offyce with his heed kembed & so to his soverayne that he be not reckeles & se that he have a clene sherte breche petycote and doublet. . . . And at morne whan your soverayne wyll aryse warme his shert by the fyre.' After directions as to dressing and washing his sovereign, the chamberlain is ordered to 'take your leve manerly & go to the chyrche or chapell to your soveraynes closet & laye carpentes & cuysshens & lay downe his boke of prayers'. He is then to return and make the bed, '& bete the federbedde & the bolster, but loke ye waste no feders.' After this 'se the hous of hesement be swete & clene & the prevy borde covered with a grene clothe and a cuysshyn'. Later on, after putting the sovereign to bed, 'dryve out dogge or catte & loke there be basyn and urynall set nere your soverayne, then take your leve manerly that your soverayne may take his rest meryly.'

The book ends with the duties of the marshal and the usher who have to order the precedence of guests.

1539 THE TREASURE OF POORE MEN.

This little book of 44 leaves contains recipes for aqua vitae and claret, but is mainly medical.

1539 THE CASTEL OF HELTHE,

gathered, and made by Sir Thomas Elyot knight, out of the chief authors of Phisyke, whereby every man may knowe the state of his owne body, the preservation of helthe, and how to instruct well his phisition in sicknes, that he be not deceyved. MDXXXIX.

This is not a cookery book, but contains advice as to the uses and physical effects of different articles of diet. According to the D.N.B. the author incurred the wrath of the physicians for encroaching on their domain.

1545 A PROPER NEWE BOOKE OF COKERYE,
declarynge what maner of meates be beste in season, for al times in the yere, and how they ought to be dressed, and served at the table, both for fleshe dayes, and fyshe dayes. With a newe addition, verye necessarye for all them that delyghteth in Cokerye.

The earliest known edition, which bears no date, is in the library of Corpus Christi College, Cambridge. It was printed by 'John Kynge and Thomas Marche'. It is a small book of 16 leaves; A to B in eights, B_8 blank. A reprint has recently been edited by Miss C. F. Frere.

Ames and Herbert (iii. 256) give an edition of 1545, printed with Richard Lant, and Hazlitt gives one of 1546, printed by Richard Lant and Richard Bankes.

The British Museum has editions of 1575 (printed by William How for Abraham Veale) and of 1576 (printed for Antony Kytson).

Maunsell gives 'A LITTLE OLDE BOOKE OF COOKERIE', printed by Antony Kytson, and Ames and Herbert (iii. 571) give 'A NEWE BOKE OF COKERY', printed by Thomas Raynald. Perhaps these are editions of the same book, but the latter would be an early edition between 1540 and 1550.

Some of the recipes are strange—A tart of Bourage Flowers, A pye of aloes (not so alarming as it seems from the title), A tart of Marygoldes, Primroses, or Cowslips, A tart of Spinage, To make egges in mone shine.

1558 THE SECRETES OF THE REVERENDE MAISTER ALEXIS OF PIEMONT.
Containyng excellente remedies against divers diseases, woundes, and other accidents, with the manner to make distilations, parfumes, confitures, diynges, colours, fusions and meltynges. A worke well approved, verye profytable

and necessary for every man. Translated out of French into English, by Wyllyam Warde.

Imprynted at London by John Kingstone for Nicolas Inglande, dwellinge in Poules Churchyarde. Anno 1558. Menss. Novemb.

This contains recipes for making ipocras, confitures, &c.

1562 Here foloweth A COMPEDYOUS REGYMENT OR A DYETARY OF HELTH, made in Moñtpylior: compiled by Andrewe Boorde, of Physicke Doctor.

The earliest edition has no date, the next is dated 1562. This book, like Elyot's Castle of Health, is not a cookery book, but gives advice as to the use of food. The author was a man of most varied experiences, not always reputable though he had once been a bishop.

1573 THE TREASURIE OF COMMODIOUS CONCEITES, AND HIDDEN SECRETS.

Commonly called The Good Huswives Closet of provision for the health of her houshold.

Meete and necessarie for the profitable use of all estates, gathered out of sundry Experiments lately practised by men of great knowledge.

The earliest known copy has lost its title-page, but the colophon is, 'These Bookes are to be sould at the West ende of Paules Church: By Richard Jones, the Printer hereof, 1573.' It is a small 12° book.

The British Museum has an edition of 1584, 'the fourth tyme corrected and inlayed, with divers necessary and new editions,' and one of 1586. The Bodleian has an edition of 1591, and Hazlitt mentions editions of 1580, 1586, 1594, and 1596.

The book is by John Partridge, of whose history nothing seems known, and it cost four pence. It is dedicated to 'Master Richard Wistow, one of the Assistants of the Companie of the Barbers and Surgeons'.

One of the most striking features of the book is the number of conserves it gives and their virtues. Thus the conserve of strawberries is 'good against a hote liver, burning of the stomacke, and specially in the fervent heat of an ague', the conserve of buglosse flowers 'comforteth the hote heart', the conserve of borage flowers

' is especially good against black choller or Melancholie, it also maketh one merie '.

There are recipes for a ' powder to make the belly soluble, causing a gentle laske : meete for Noble personages ', ' To make the face fayre and the breath sweete ', ' To make haire as yellow as gold ', ' To make Manus Christi '.

The book next appears as a quarto with a somewhat different title :

THE TREASURIE OF HIDDEN SECRETS.

Commonlie called, The good-huswives Closet of provision, for the health of her Houshold.

Gathered out of sundry experiments, lately practised by men of great knowledge : And now newly enlarged, with divers necessary Phisicke helpes, and knowledge of the names and naturall disposition of diseases, that most commonly happen to men and women.

Not impertinent for every good Huswife to use in her house, amongst her owne familie.

At London, printed by J R for Edward White, and are to be sold at his shop at the little North doore of Paules, at the signe of the Gunne, 1600.

It is a thin quarto, A to I in fours. It was reprinted twice in 1627 and again in 1633, 1637, and 1653. Professor Ferguson gives an edition of 1656.

1574 A DIRECTION FOR THE HEALTH OF MAGISTRATES AND STUDENTES.

Namely suche as bee in their consistent Age, or neere thereunto : Drawen as well out of sundry good and commendable Authours, as also upon reason and faithfull experience otherwise certaynely grounded. Written in Latin by Gulielmus Gratarolus, and Englished by T. N.

Imprinted at London, in Fleete streete, by William How, for Abraham Veale, 1574.

This is not a cookery book, but merely contains advice as to the use of food. Gratarolus was an Italian who was compelled to leave his country on account of his having embraced the Calvinist faith.

He practised physic at Bâle, and died in 1568. Thomas Newton, the translator, was Rector of Little Ilford.

1582 A COMPENDIUM OF THE RATIONALL SECRETES

of the worthie Knight and moste excellent Doctour of Phisicke and Chirurgerie, Leonardo Phioravante Bolognese, divided into three Bookes.

In the first is shewed many secretes apperteinyng unto Phisicke.

In the seconde is shewed many secretes apperteining unto Chirurgerie, with their uses.

In the third is shewed divers compositions, apperteinyng bothe to Phisicke and Chirurgerie, with the hidden vertues of sondrie vegitables, anumalles, and mineralls, and proved wel by this Authour, hetherto never set out before.

Imprinted at London by Jhon Kyngston, for George Pen, and I. H., 1582.

Fioravante died at Bologna in 1588. The translator of the book was John Hester, of whom there is an account in the D. N. B. The cookery receipts are in Book III. Curious pieces of information are given, e.g. 'Take a Capon and pull awaie all his feathers from his breaste, and beate hym with Nettles, and he will call in the young Chickens, and governe them like the Henne.'

1583 THE SCHOOLEMASTER

or Teacher of Table Philosophie. A most pleasant and merie Companion, well worthy to be welcomed (for a dayly Gheast) not onelye to all mens hoorde, to guide them with moderate and holsome dyet; but also into every mans Companie at all tymes, to recreat their mindes, with honest mirth and delectable devises to sundry pleasant purposes of pleasure and pastyme.

Gathered out of divers, the best approved Aucthors:

And devided into foure pithy and pleasant Treatises, as it may appeare by the contentes.

Imprinted at London, by Richard Johnes dwelling at the

Signe of the Rose and the Crown, neere Holburne Bridge. 1583.

The first Booke of Table Philosophie treateth of the nature and qualitie of all manner meates, drinkes, and Sauces that are used at meales.

The second Booke of Table Philosophie which speaketh of the maners, behaviour, and usadge of all sutch with whome wee may happen to be conversaunt at the Table.

The third Booke of Table Philosophie which containeth certen delectable and pleasant Questions, to bee propounded for mirth while we be at meate or at any other time.

The fourth Booke of Table Philosophie which compriseth many merry honest Jestes, delectable devyses and pleasant purposes, to be for delight and recreation at the boord among Company.

This book was written by Thomas Twyne, a doctor of Lewes, or Thomas Turswell, a Canon of St. Paul's. The D. N. B. suggests that the 'honest Jestes' were hardly such as could be dedicated by a canon to his dean. The D. N. B. mentions an edition of 1576.

1585 (?) THE GOOD HUSWIFES JEWELL.

Wherein is to be found most excellent and rare Devises for conceites in Cookery, found out by the practise of Thomas Dawson.

Whereunto is adjoyned sundry approved receits for many soveraine oyles, and the way to distill many precious waters, with divers approved medicines for many diseases.

Also certain approved points of husbandry, very necessary for all Husbandmen to know.

Newly set foorth with additions, 1596.

Imprinted at London for Edward White dwelling at the Little North doore of Paules at the signe of the Gun.

This is a 12º of 52 leaves. The head-line is 'A Booke of Cookerie'. No earlier edition than 1596 seems known. Watt mentions an undated edition, and Hazlitt one of 1610. The book was reprinted

8 ENGLISH COOKERY BOOKS

in 1620 under the title of 'A Booke of Cookerie'. The book tells one how 'To make muggets', 'To make a mortis', 'To make a Blewmanger'. A cure for obesity is likely to do quite as much good as the modern quack remedies. 'To make one slender. Take Fennell, and seeth it in Water, a very good quantity, and wringing out the juyce thereof when it is sodde, drink it first and last, and it shall swage either man or woman.'

1585 THE SECOND PART OF THE GOOD HUS-WIFES JEWELL,

Wherein is to bee found most apt and readiest wayes to distill many wholsome and sweete waters,

In which likewise is shewed the best manner in preserving of divers sorts of Fruites, and making of Syrropes:

With divers Conseites in Cookerie after the Italian and French maner.

Never the like published by any untill this present yere, 1585.

Imprinted at London for Edward White, dwelling at the little North doore of Paules Church, at the signe of the Gunne.

Another edition of 1597 has added to it 'The Book of Carving'. Maunsell gives an edition of 1590, and Hazlitt one of 1606. The book is similar to the first part and has 72 pages. The head-line is 'A Booke of Cookerie'. In the 1597 edition, 'The Booke of Carving and Sewing' has a separate title-page and is unpaged.

There are recipes 'To make Pursses or Cremitaries',—this begins 'Take a little Mary'—'To make Jombrils', 'To make a Colluce', 'To make a Condonacke'.

1586 THE OLDE MANS DIETARIE.

A worke no lesse learned then necessary for the preservation of Olde persons in perfect health and soundnesse.

Englished out of Latine, and now first published by Thomas Newton.

Imprinted at London for Edward White, dwelling at the little North-doore of Sainct Paules Church, at the signe of the Gun. 1586.

This book, like the one of Gratarolus which Newton also translated, is not a cookery book, but gives advice as to the use of foods.

1588 THE HOUSEHOLDERS PHILOSOPHIE,

Wherein is perfectly & profitably described, the true Oeconomia and forme of Housekeeping, with a Table added thereunto of all the notable things therein contained.

First written in Italian by that excellent Orator and Poet, Signior Torquato Tasso, and now translated by T. K.

Whereunto is annexed a dairie Booke for all good huswives.

At London, printed by F. C. for Thomas Hacket, and are to be sold at his shop in Lomberd streete under the signe of the Popes head, M D LXXXVIII.

This is a set of rules and regulations ; there are no recipes. The original, Il Padre di Famiglia, was published in 1583.

1588 THE GOOD HOUS-WIVES TREASURIE.

Beeing a verye necessarie Booke instructing to the dressing of Meates.

Hereunto is also annexed sundrie holsome Medicines for divers diseases.

Imprinted at London by Edward Allde, 1588.

This is a small 12° which gives recipes ' How to make a Florentine ', ' How to make Dousets ', ' For a Tansie ', ' How to make a Cullis for a sick body,' &c.

1591 A BOOK OF COOKRYE.

Very necessary for all such as delight therin.

Gathered by A. W.

And now newlye enlarged, with the serving in of the Table.

With the proper Sauces to each of them convenient.

At London, printed by Edward Allde, 1591.

This is in the Bodleian ; a reprint of 1594 is in the B. M. It tells how ' To boyle a Cony with a pudding in his belly ', ' To still a Cocke for a weake body that is consumed ', ' How to make a pudding in a Turnip roote ', ' A pudding in a Cowcumber ', ' How to make Chuets ', ' How to make a Tarte of Brier hips ', ' To make Bennets '.

1594 THE GOOD HUSWIFES HANDMAIDE FOR THE KITCHIN.

Containing manie principall pointes of Cookerie, as well how to dresse meates, after sundrie the best fashions used in England and other Countries, with their apt and proper sawces, both for flesh and fish, as also the orderly serving of the same to the Table.

Hereunto are annexed, sundrie necessarie Conceits for the preservation of health.

Verie meete to be adjoined to the good Huswifes Closet of provision for her Houshold.

Imprinted at London by Richard Jones, 1594.

This little 12° of 55 leaves is in the Bodleian. According to Maunsell the first edition was printed by Richard Jones and Ant. Hyll in 1588. The head-line is 'A New Booke of Cookerie'.

It gives three ways of preserving lard: 'How to keep Lard after my Lord Ferries way', 'How to keepe Larde after my Lady Westone Brownes way', 'The keeping of Lard after my Lady Marquesse Dorsets way'. There are recipes for 'A tart to provoke courage either in man or woman', 'To make good Restons', 'How to make a Vaunt', 'The making of fine manchet'.

A BOOKE OF COOKERIE,

Otherwise called: The good Huswives Handmaid for the kitchin.

Wherein is shewed the order how to dresse meates after sundry the best fashions used in England and other Countries: with their apt and proper sauces both for flesh and fish: as also the orderly serving the same to the Table.

Whereunto are annexed sundry necessary Conceites for the preservation of health.

London, printed by E. Allde, dwelling in Aldersgate streete, over-against the Pump, 1597.

This is the same book as the last with a new title. The head-line is 'A New Booke of Cookerie'.

THE GOOD HUSWIVES HANDMAID, FOR COOKERIE in her Kitchin, &c.

The book under this title in the B.M. is the same as the last. It has lost its title-page, and A₂ and the name has been taken from the half-title.

1595 THE WIDDOWES TREASURE.

Plentifully furnished with sundry precious and approved secrets in Phisicke and Chirurgery, for the health and pleasure of Mankinde.

Heereunto are adjoyned, sundrie prittie practices and conclusions of Cookerie, with many profitable and wholsome Medicines, for sundrie diseases in Cattell.

At London, printed by J. Roberts for Edward White, 1595.

There were editions of 1631 and 1639; the former is in the Bodleian.

In a preface signed M. R. the book is said to have been written 'at the earnest request and sute of a Gentlewoman in the Country for her private use, which by these singular practices hath obtained such fame, that her name shall bee remembered for ever to the Posterity'. In spite of the preface it is difficult to believe that a gentlewoman could have treated or even described so plainly some of the diseases mentioned. The book has no arrangement of subjects. Thus five consecutive recipes are, 'To keepe Venison from rotting ', 'To keepe Peares ', 'To kill Lice ', 'Against drunkennesse', 'To make Linnen Cloth, or Yarne white '. A recipe for 'Diatrion Piperion ', made of pepper, time, ginger, aniseeds, &c., moves the author or authoress to poetry.

> Virtutis hujus confectionis sequuntur.
> This decoction is good to eate
>   alwaies before and after meate.
> For it will make digestion good,
>   and turne your meate to pure blood.
> Besides all this it dooth excell,
>   all windines to expell.
> And all groce humors colde and rawe,
>   that are in belly, stomacke or mawe
> It will dissolve without paine,
>   and keepe ill vapors from the braine.
> Besides all this it will restore
>   Your memory though lost before.
> Use it therefore when you please,
>   for therein resteth mighty ease.

1595 (?) A THOUSAND NOTABLE THINGS
of sundry sorts, &c.

This book, by Thomas Lupton, is almost entirely medical. There are many editions of it, one as late as 1815. The earliest, undated but about 1595, was 'imprinted at London by John Charlewood, for Hughe Spooner, dwelling in Lumbardstreete at the signe of the Cradle'.

1598 EPULARIO,
or The Italian Banquet:
Wherein is shewed the maner how to dresse and prepare all kind of Flesh, Foules, or Fishes.
As also how to make Sauces, Tartes, Pies, etc. After the maner of all Countries.
With an addition of many other profitable and necessary things.
Translated out of Italian into English.
London, printed by A. J. for William Bailey, and are to bee sold at his shop in Gratious street neere Leaden-hall, 1598.

This is a translation of a book by Giovanne de Rosselli. The original first appeared in 1516, according to Brunet.

There is a recipe 'To make pies that the Birds may be alive in them, and flie out when it is cut up', and another horrid one 'To make Pies of the Combes of Cockes and Hennes, with their stones, and livers', the other ingredients being cherries, sinamon, ginger, saffron, and vergiuice.

1599 DYETS DRY DINNER:
Consisting of eight severall Courses:

- 1. Fruites.
- 2. Hearbes.
- 3. Flesh.
- 4. Fish.
- 5. Whitmeats.
- 6. Spice.
- 7. Sauce.
- 8. Tabacco.

All served in after the order of Time universall.
By Henry Buttes, Maister of Artes, and Fellowe of C.C.C. in C.
Qui miscuit utile Dulci.
       CICERO.

Non nobis solum nati sumus, sed ortus nostri sibi vendicant. Printed in London by Tho. Creede, for William Wood, and are to be sold at the West end of Powles, at the signe of Tyme, 1599.

This is not a cookery book, but a description of different articles of food on one side of the page and a 'story for table-talke' about each on the other. Some of the stories could certainly not be told at modern dinner-tables. There is an account of the author in Robert Masters's History of Corpus Christi College. Buttes was elected master of the college in 1626 and vice-chancellor in 1629. ' He being to preach before the university as vice-chancellor on Easter-day, April 1. 1632, was found hanging in his garters in his own chamber.' There is a portrait of him in the master's lodge. Lowndes states that there is a portrait of him in Harding's Biographical Mirror, but this seems to be a mistake.

1600 NATURALL AND ARTIFICIAL DIRECTIONS

for health, derived from the best Philosophers, as well moderne, as aunciert.

By William Vaughan, Master of Artes, and Student in the Civill Law.

London, printed by Richard Bradocke, 1600.

Part of this book is on the use of foods. The author, who lived from 1577 to 1641, helped to colonize Newfoundland. 1602 (2), 1607 (3), 1617 (5), 1626 (6), 1633 (7).

1600 (?) DELIGHTES FOR LADIES,

To adorne their Persons, Tables, Closets, and Distillatories ; with Beauties, Banquets, Perfumes, & Waters.

Reade, Practice, & Censure.

At London, printed by Peter Short.

A most charming little book within borders, in some of which are woven the initials E R. It consists of A to H in twelves, H_{12} being a blank leaf with borders. A rhymed epistle is signed H. Plat. The book was reprinted in 1602, 1608, 1609, 1611, 1615, 1630, 1632, 1636. Later editions, 1647, 1651, 1654, 1656, 1683, are printed without the borders. Hazlitt gives editions of 1600, 1603, 1618, 1640. Hugh Plat, the son of a London brewer, was born in 1552, and knighted in 1605 as a reward for his literary efforts.

ENGLISH COOKERY BOOKS

The recipes seem as charming as the book itself. 'The most kindly waie to preserve plums', 'To make a paste to keepe you moist, if you list not to drinke oft, which Ladies use to carry with them when they ride abroad', 'To candie Orange pilles', 'To make a cullis as white as snowe, and in the nature of gellie', 'Usquebash or Irish Aqua vitae', 'a Scottish handwater'.

1607 THE ENGLISHMAN'S DOCTER, OR THE SCHOOLE OF SALERNE,

or, Physicall observations for the perfect Preserving of the body of Man in continuall Health.

London : Printed for John Helme, and John Busby Junior, and are to be solde at the little shoppe, next Clifford's Inne gate, in Fleet-streete. 1607.

This is the earliest translation of the famous Latin poem said to have been written by the physicians of Salerno for the preservation of the health of Robert, eldest son of William the Conqueror. The commentary, written by Arnaldus de Villa Nova, who died about 1313, was translated as early as 1528 by T. Paynell. The poem is concerning the use of foods. Among other editions there is one of 1634 'whereunto is annexed a necessary Discourse of all sorts of Fish in use among us, with their effects, appertayning to the health of Man'.

1608 A CLOSET FOR LADIES AND GENTLEWOMEN,

or, The Art of preserving, Conserving, and Candying.

With the manner howe to make divers kinds of Syrups : and all kind of banqueting stuffes.

Also divers soveraigne Medicines and Salves, for sundry Diseases.

At London, printed for Arthur Johnson, dwelling neere the great North dore of Pauls, 1608.

12°; A to M in eights ; pages 1-190. A little book within borders, much resembling 'Delightes for Ladies' by Plat, to whom the book is attributed in the Douce catalogue, but it looks more like a rival work.

The book was reprinted in 1611, and again in 1630, 1632, and 1636 with different borders. An edition of 1647 has a portrait of a lady as frontispiece, but no borders. Later editions of 1651, 1654, and 1656 have a table of contents, but no portrait and no borders. Hazlitt gives an edition of 1635. This book contains many tempting recipes. 'To make a Walnut, that when you cracke it, you shall find Biskets, and Carrawayes in it, or a prettie Posey written.' 'To make an excellent Marmelate which was given Queene Mary for a New-yeares gift.' 'To make another sort of Marmelate very comfortable and restorative for any Lord or Lady whatsoever.' The following seems to be the remedy of the day for appendicitis. 'For one that is taken within the body, or any place. Take Rose cakes, aqua-vitae, and rose water, heate it on a chafindish of coales, lay it to the stomacke, they shall mend by God's grace.'

1614 THE PHILOSOPHERS BANQUET;

newly furnished and decked forth with much variety of many severall Dishes, that in the former Service were neglected. Where now not onely Meates and Drinks of all Natures and Kindes are served in, but the Names and Kindes of all disputed of. — — — —

The second Edition, newly corrected and inlarged, to almost as much more. By W. B. Esquire.

London, printed by T. C. for Leonard Becket, and are to bee solde at his shoppe in the Temple, neere the Church. 1614.

The first edition of this book was entered in the Stationers' Register of May 29, 1609, but no copy is known. The book, which is on the uses of foods and on many other topics, is famous for being the first to contain a quotation from Hamlet. The third edition was printed for Nicholas Vavasour in 1633. The original, Mensa Philosophica, of which the first known edition is 1475, has been ascribed both to Sir Michael Scott and to Theobald Anguilbert, an Irish physician. According to a note in one of Sotheby's catalogues W. B. was probably the same person who published the 'Court of Good Counsel' in 1607, 'A Help to Discourse' in 1619, and a paraphrase of the tenth satire of Juvenal in 1617. Part of 'A Help to Discourse' is from 'The Philosophers Banquet'.

1615 THE ENGLISH HUS-WIFE,

Contayning, The inward and outward vertues which ought to be in a compleat woman.

As, her skill in Physicke, Cookery, Banqueting-stuffe,

Distillation, Perfumes, Wooll, Hemp, Flax, Dayries, Brewing, Baking, and all other things belonging to an Houshould.

A Worke very profitable and necessarie, gathered for the generall good of this kingdome.

Printed at London by John Beale, for Roger Jackson, and are to bee sold at his shop neere the great Conduit in Fleetstreete, 1615.

This is the second book of 'Countrey Contentments', by Gervase Markham, who was born about 1568 and died in 1637. He has been called 'the earliest English hackney writer'. Other editions are 1623, 1631 (4), 1637 (5), 1648, 1649, 1656 (6), 1660 (7), 1664, 1668 (8), 1675, 1683 (9). An edition of 1653 was reprinted by Constance, Countess De La Warr, in 1907.

The cookery recipes seem more modern than those of preceding books, although many of the dishes are obsolete, e.g. leach and jumbal. The medical recipes, however, are appalling, animal dung and other filth being frequent ingredients.

1617 A DAILY EXERCISE FOR LADIES AND GENTLEWOMEN.

Whereby they may learne and practise the whole Art of making Pastes, Preserves, Marmalades, Conserves, Tart-stuffes, Gellies, Breads, Sucket-Candies, Cordiall waters, Conceits in Sugar-workes of several kindes.

As also to dry Lemons, Orenges, or other Fruits.

Newly set forth, according to the now approved Receipts, used both by Honourable and Worshipfull personages.

By John Murrel Professor thereof.

London : printed for the widow Helme, and are to be sould at her shop in S. Dunstans Church-yard in Fleet street, 1617.

This is a pretty little book [1] printed within borders ; A to G in twelves, A_1, G_{11}, and G_{12} being blank. After the table of contents is a preface—'Gentle Reader, if any shall bee desirous to buy any of the moulds wherein any of the formes specified in the Booke following are made, they may have them also where these Bookes

---

[1] This is a very rare book. I bought a copy at Sotheby's in 1904 for £10 5s., and some time after a copy was sent me for four shillings. These are the only copies I have seen.

are to be sould. Farewell.' The recipes begin with ' To make Paste of Regia against a Consumption ', but most of the others look delightful. ' To make rough red marmalade of Quinces, commonly called lump-Marmalade, that shall looke as red as any Rubie ', ' To make red Marmalade of Pippins, orient and cleare ', ' To make Dia Setonia of Quinces, a cordiall for the stomack ', ' To make Conserve of Cowslips, good against Melancholy ', ' To make Quiddoniock ', ' To make an excellent Bread called Ginetoes ', ' To make Aqua-Coelestis ', ' To make Letters, Knots, or any other Jumball for a banquet quicklie '. Towards the end are recipes for making such strange things as ' Pennet ', ' Callishones ', ' Muscachones ', ' Muscadinoes, commonly called kissing-Comfits ', ' Canalones ', ' Rushilians ', ' Gentilissoes ', and ' Novellissoes '.

1617 A NEW BOOK OF COOKERIE.

Wherein is set forth a most perfect direction to furnish an extraordinary, or ordinary feast, either in Summer or Winter.

Also a Bill of Fare for Fish-dayes, Fasting dayes, Emberweekes, or Lent.

And likewise the most commendable fashion of Dressing, or Sowcing, either Flesh, Fish, or Fowle : for making of Gellies, and other Made-dishes for service, to beautifie either Noblemans or Gentlemans Table.

Together with the newest fashion of cutting up any Fowle.

Hereunto also is added the most exquisite English Cookerie. All set forth according to the now, new, English and French fashion.

By John Murrell.

London, printed for John Browne, and are to be sould at his Shop in Dunstanes Church-yard, 1617.

The book (A to H_3 in eights, A_1 being blank) begins with the dishes for various courses at a feast. Some recipes seem new, e. g. ' To smoore an old Coney, Ducke, or Mallard on the French fashion ', ' To make Pancakes so crispe that you may set them upright ', ' A sallet of rose-buds and clove gilly-flowers ', ' A fierced pudding ', ' A fond pudding '.

1620 A BOOKE OF COOKERIE.
And the order of Meates to bee served to the Table, both for Flesh and Fish dayes.

With many excellent wayes for the dressing of all usuall sortes of meates, both Bak't, boyld, or rosted, of Flesh, fish, Fowle, or others, with their proper sawces.

As also many rare Inventions in Cookery for made Dishes; with most notable preserves of sundry sorts of Fruits. Likewise for making many precious Waters, with divers approved Medicines for grievous diseases.

With certaine points of Husbandry how to Order Oxen, Horses, Sheepe, Hogges, &c., with many other necessary points for Husbandmen to know.

London, printed by Edw. All-de, dwelling neere Christ-Church, 1620.

This is merely an abbreviated edition of Thomas Dawson's Good Huswifes Jewell. It was reprinted in this form in 1629, 1634, and 1650.

1620 VIA RECTA AD VITAM LONGAM ...
. . by Tobias Venner, Doctor of Physicke, at Bathe in the Spring, and Fall, . . .

London. Printed by Edward Griffin for Richard Moore, and are to be sold at his shop in St. Dunstans Church-yard in Fleet-street. 1620.

Other editions are 1622 (2), 1628, 1638, 1650, 1660 (4). It is a book on the uses of foods. Venner lived from 1577 to 1660.

1621 A DELIGHTFULL DAILY EXERCISE FOR LADIES AND GENTLEWOMEN.
Whereby is set foorth the secrete misteries of the purest preservings in Glasses and other Confrictionaries, as making of Breads, Pastes, Preserves, Suckets, Marmalates, Tartstuffes, rough Candies, and many other things never before in Print. Whereto is added a Booke of Cookery.

ENGLISH COOKERY BOOKS

By John Murrell Professor thereof.

London, printed for Tho. Dewe, and are to be sold at his shoppe in St. Dunstons Church-yard in Fleete-street, 1621.

In the course of his preface ' To all ladies and gentlewomen, and others whatsoever ', the author speaks of this book as ' an Addition to my former practise which I did attaine unto in my travels when I was in France, Italy, the Low-Countries, and divers other places '. He speaks of his craft as ' Art and Mistery '.

The book is printed within borders. The first part of it is A to G_1 in twelves, A_1 being blank ; there are one or two misprints, e. g. A instead of B. The book of cookery has a separate title-page, and consists of A with 8 leaves, B with 12, C with 5 ; it is a reprint of the edition of 1617.

The recipes of the ' Delightful Daily Exercise ' are much like those of the ' Daily Exercise '. ' To sucket candy greene Lemons, a very cordial thing for the Stomake ', ' To make Premellies ', ' To make Oring chipps, a very cordial thing against the paine or wind in the stomacke ', ' To fry an egge as round as a ball '. There are plans of how sweets are to be arranged on the table.

1631 MURRELS TWO BOOKES OF COOKERIE AND CARVING.

The fourth time printed with new Additions.

London, printed by M. F. for John Marriot, and are to be sold at his Shop in Saint Dunstans Church-yard in Fleet street, 1631.

Each book has its separate title-page, and at the end is ' A New Booke of Carving and Sewing ',[1] which also has its own title-page. The preface is dated July 20, 1630. In it the author disparages previous cookery books, ' the most of which nevertheless have instructed rather how to marre than make good Meate.'

The fifth edition was 1638, the sixth 1641, and the seventh 1650.

There are not many new recipes in the book. One pleasant one is ' To bake a Quince or a Warden pie, so as the fruit may be redde, and the crust pale and tender '. At the very end is ' An excellent and much approved receit, for a long Consumption '. It consists of white snails kept in wine and then boiled in milk with sugar. ' This being duely made and taken accordingly, will with God's helpe recover the party being very weake and farre spent in this long lingering sicknesse.'

[1] See p. 2.

1633 KLINIKH OR THE DIET OF THE DISEASED.
Divided into Three Bookes, &c., &c.
Newly published by James Hart, Doctor in Physicke.
London, printed by John Beale, for Robert Allot, and are to be sold at his shop at the signe of the black Beare in Pauls Church-yard, 1633.

> This is a curious book with a strong Protestant bias. The author practised at Northampton. It is the earliest book on the subject in the English language, but a German one by Ryff was published at Frankfort in 1545.

1634 THE MYSTERYES OF NATURE AND ART:
Conteined in foure severall Tretises, The first of water workes, The second of Fyer workes, The third of Drawing, Colouring, Painting, and Engraving, The fourth of divers Experiments, as wel serviceable as delightful; partly collected, and partly of the Author's Peculiar Practise, and Invention by J. B.
Imprinted for Ralph Mab, 1634.

> There are a few receipts in the fourth book. By John Bate.

1634 HYGIASTICON:
or, The right course of preserving Life and Health unto extream old Age; Together with soundnesse and integritie of the Senses, Judgement, and Memorie. Written in Latine by Leonard Lessius, and now done into English.
The second Edition.
Printed by the Printers to the Universitie of Cambridge, 1634.

> A book on the uses of foods. The first edition of the original was 1613. Another translation of the book, by 'Timothy Smith, Apothecary', was published in 1743.
>
> At the beginning of the 1634 edition is 'A Dialogue between a Glutton and Echo', which begins:
>
> > My belly I do deifie.
> > Fie.
> > Who curbs his appetite 's a fool.
> > Ah fool.

1639 THE LADIES CABINET OPENED:
Wherein is found hidden severall Experiments in Preserving and Conserving, Physicke, and Surgery, Cookery and Huswifery.

London, printed by M. P. for Richard Meighen, next to the Middle Temple in Fleet street, 1639.

This is the original edition of the following book:

THE LADIES CABINET ENLARGED AND OPENED:
Containing Many Rare Secrets, and Rich Ornaments of several kindes, and different uses.

Comprized under three general Heads.

viz., of
1. Preserving, Conserving, Candying, &c.
2. Physick and Chirurgery.
3. Cookery and Housewifery.

Whereunto is added, Sundry Experiments, and Choice Extractions of Waters, Oyls, &c.

Collected and practised by the late Right Honorable and Learned Chymist, the Lord Ruthven.

With a particular Table to each Part.

London, printed by T. M. for M. M., G. Bedell, and T. Collins, at the middle Temple Gate, Fleet-street, 1654.

The first book is a quarto (A to H in fours), the second a duodecimo (A 4 leaves, then A to K_8 in twelves, followed by 6 leaves of L, which are occupied by advertisements). The second edition was 1655, the third 1658, the fourth 1667. There is an account of the book in Notes and Queries, Second Series, vol. ii, 264, 333. The preface to The Ladies Cabinet Enlarged and Opened is signed M. B. There are recipes ' To make the fine Bisket Bread, called in some places Norffe-Cakes, and commonly Diet-bread ', ' To make Veal Tootes or Olives ', and some odd medical prescriptions, ' The purge of Assarabacha, which the Lady A. D. used to rectifie her stomacke, any wayes offended ', ' a receit for a backward businesse '.

1649 A PRECIOUS TREASURY OF TWENTY RARE SECRETS,
Most Necessary, Pleasant, and Profitable for all sorts of People.

Published by La Fountaine, an Expert Operator.
London, printed Anno Dom. 1649.

This is a quarto of 4 leaves with a few cookery recipes. It is reprinted in a book of the same date by Salvator Winter [1] of Naples and Francisco Dickinson, and ascribed to Dickinson. All three were quacks who at the end of their books advertised their residence and their ability to 'pull out all manner of Hollow Teeth, stumps or roots, with great dexterity and ease, without almost any paine'.

1652 A HERMETICALL BANQUET,
drest by a Spagiricall Cook: for the better Preservation of the Microcosme.
London, printed for Andrew Crooke, and are to be sold at the Green Dragon in S. Pauls Church-yard. 1652.

This is a queer medical book, but contains a few cookery recipes.

1653 A) A CHOICE MANUALL,
of Rare and Select Secrets in Physick and Chirurgery: collected, and practised by the Right Honourable, the Countesse of Kent, late deceased.
As also most Exquisite ways of Preserving, Conserving, Candying, &c.
Published by W. J. Gent.
London, printed by R. Norton, 1653.

B) A TRUE GENTLEWOMANS DELIGHT,
Wherein is contained all manner of Cookery:

Together with { Preserving, Conserving, Drying, and Candying,

Very necessary for all Ladies and Gentlewomen.
Published by W. J., Gent.
London, printed by R. Norton, 1653.

These two books, by the same author (W. Jar.), seem to have been issued together, though the pagination is distinct and occa-

---

[1] Winter is mentioned in Digby's Choice and Experimented Receipts, 148.

ENGLISH COOKERY BOOKS

sionally one book is seen without the other. The lettering of the sheets is also distinct in the first edition and in one imprint of the second edition, but in other editions it is continuous. The book is a small octavo in size; A with 4 leaves, B to F_3 in twelves, followed by A with 4 leaves, B to E_4 in twelves. The copy in the British Museum looks of much later date than subsequent editions, which are of a small duodecimo size, but there was a Roger Norton printer from 1639 to 1662, so that it is difficult to regard it as a reprint. The second edition was 1653, of which there are two imprints. Other editions are 1658 (10), 1659 (11), 1661, 1663 (14), 1667 (15), 1682 (18), 1687 (19), 1708. Professor Ferguson gives the 4th edition as 1654, and the 12th as 2659 (*sic*). He also notes an edition of 1656.

There is a portrait of the Countess of Kent as frontispiece to all the editions except the first, and it may be mentioned that the book is catalogued under her name, Elizabeth Grey, in the British Museum. She was second daughter of Gilbert Talbot, Earl of Shrewsbury, and wife of Henry de Grey, Earl of Kent. She died at Whitefriars on December 7, 1751.[1]

The first book is purely medical, and recommends the usual filthy remedies, e. g. the dung of a peacock for convulsions and powdered earthworms for jaundice. It gives 'A cordiall for the Sea. Take one ounce of Sirupe of Clove-gilliflowers, one drachm of Confectio Alchermes, one ounce and a half of Borrage water, and the like of Mint-water, one ounce of Mr. Mountfords water, and as much of Cinnamon-water, temper all these together in a Cordial, and take a spoonful at a time when you are at sea '. The second book is the cookery part, and tells how to make a slipcoat Cheese, Angellets, fine Diet-bread, Essings, Ponado, Bonny Clutter, Lady of Arundels Manchet, &c.

1653 THE FRENCH COOK.

Prescribing the way of making ready of all sorts of Meats, Fish and Flesh, with the proper Sauces, either to procure Appetite, or to advance the power of Digestion.

Also the Preparation of all Herbs and Fruits, so as their naturall Crudities are by art opposed; with the whole skil of Pastry-work.

Together with a Treatise of Conserves, both dry and liquid, a la mode de France.

---

[1] Walpole's Royal and Noble Authors, 1806, iii. 44; Granger's Biographical History, 1824, iii. 209.

With an Alphabeticall Table explaining the hard words, and other usefull Tables.

Written in French by Monsieur De La Varenne, Clerk of the Kitchin to the Lord Marquesse of Uxelles, and now Englished by I. D. G.

London, printed for Charles Adams, and are to be sold at his Shop, at the Sign of the Talbot neere St. Dunstans Church in Fleetstreet, 1653.

This is a translation of *Le Cuisinier françois*, which ran through many editions in the original. There is a frontispiece representing a cook in his kitchen. The second edition (1654) also contains it, but it is omitted in the third [1] (1673), which is of larger size than the previous editions. This is the first cookery book which has any order and arrangement in its contents.

1653 A BOOK OF FRUITS AND FLOWERS.

Shewing the Nature and Use of them, either for Meat or Medicine. As also to Preserve, Conserve, Candy, and in Wedges, or Dry them. To make Powders, Civet bagges, all sorts of Sugar-works, turn'd works in Sugar, Hollow, or Frutages ; and to Pickell them.

And for Meat.

To make Pyes, Biscat, Maid Dishes, Marchpanes, Leeches, and Snow, Craknels, Caudels, Cakes, Broths, Fritterstuffe, Puddings, Tarts, Syrupes, and Sallets.

For Medicines.

To make all sorts of Poultisses, and Serecloaths for any member swell'd or inflamed, Ointments, Waters for all Wounds, and Cancers, Salves for Aches, to take the Ague out of any place Burning or Scalding ; for the stopping of suddain Bleeding, curing the Piles, Ulcers, Ruptures, Coughs, Consumptions, and killing of Warts, to dissolve the Stone, killing the Ring-worme, Emroids, and Dropsie, Paine in the Ears and Teeth, Deafnesse.

[1] There is a warning in this edition against 'a Counterfeit Piece in imitation thereof, by the Title of The English and French Cook ; it being only patched up by mangling and spoiling the approved Receipts of this Book '.

Contra vim mortis, non est medicamen in hortis.

London, printed by M. S. for Tho. Jenner at the South entrance of the Royall Exchange, London, 1653.

This is a small quarto of 49 pages. The last two pages are wrongly put as 50, 51 in one of the British Museum copies, but are correct in the other. There was an edition of 1656 sold at Sotheby's a few years ago. The contents of the book are curiously arranged. There is first an engraving of the fruit or flower, and then follow recipes both in medicine and cookery which contain it. Thus the first engraving is of a lemon, and among the recipes are 'a lemmon sallet', 'Past of lemmons', 'To take away the Spots, or red Pimpels of the face', 'Sweet Bagges to lay amongst Linnen', 'To roste a Shoulder of Mutton with Lemmons'.

1654 THE ART OF COOKERY.

Refin'd and Augmented, containing an Abstract of some rare and rich unpublished Receipts of Cookery : Collected from the practice of that incomparable Master of these Arts, Mr. Jos. Cooper, chiefe Cook to the late King : With severall other practises by the Author, with an addition of Preserves, Conserves, &c., offering an infallible delight to all Judicious Readers.

London, printed by F. G. for R. Lowndes at the White-lyon in St. Paul's Church-yard, neer the West end, 1654.

The preface says that the title-pages of some cookery books, 'like the contents of a weekly Pamphlet, promised much more than the Books performed,' but the only thing likely to displease ladies in this book 'will be to see so many uncommon, and undeflour'd Receipts prostituted to the publique view, which might perchance . . . have been plac'd better among the paper-secrets in a few of your Cabinets'.

There are recipes to 'fry Skerroots', 'make a Paris-pie', 'a Pie answerable to the grand boyled meat, with 10 other pies belonging to the first'.

1654 THE LADIES COMPANION,

or, A Table furnished with sundry sorts of Pies and Tarts, gracefull at a Feast, with many excellent receipts for Preserving, Conserving, and Candying of all manner of fruits,

ENGLISH COOKERY BOOKS

with the making of Marchpanes, Marmalet, and Quindenis.
By Persons of quality whose names are mentioned.

London, printed by W. Bentley, and are to be sold· by
W. Shears, at the sign of the Bible, in S. Pauls Church
yard, 1654.

The peculiarity of this little book of 82 pages is that names are attached to most of the recipes, e. g. Mrs. Medgate's Broth, Mrs. Heyden's White Broth, Mrs. Atkinson's Pudding for Fridays, The Lady Butler's Cream of Almonds, The Lady Goring's Sullybub, The Lady Throgmorton's Egg Pie.

1655 THE QUEENS CLOSET OPENED,
Incomparable Secrets in Physick, Chirurgery, Preserving
and Candying, and Cookery ; as they were presented to
the Queen, By the most experienced Persons of our Times,
many whereof were honoured with her own practice, when
she pleased to descend to these more private Recreations.
Never before published.

Transcribed from the true Copies of her Majesties own
Receipt Books, by W. M., one of her late servants.

Vivit post funera Virtus.

Printed for Nathaniel Brook at the Angel in Cornhill, 1655.

This consists of three books, 'THE PEARLE OF PRACTICE', 'A QUEENS DELIGHT', and 'THE COMPLEAT COOK', the last two having separate title-pages. 'THE COMPLEAT COOK', nearly always separately paged, was sometimes published by itself. The other two, though sometimes separately paged, seem to have been nearly always published together.

There is a portrait of Henrietta Maria Regina by Gulielmus Faithorne as frontispiece.

Other editions are 1656, 1661, 1662, 1668, 1671, 1674, 1679, 1683, 1684, 1696 (10), 1710 (11), 1713 (11). In the British Museum the book is catalogued under W. M.

A 1659 edition of ' The Compleat Cook ' was probably issued by itself, as the lettering of the sheets begins with A. One of 1664 begins with N.

The dates on the title-pages of the second and third books do not always correspond with the date of the first title-page.

The preface to the first edition begins, ' The Queens Closet opened,

To those Persons of Honour and Quality, that presented many of these admirable Receipts at the feet of the Queens Majesty, the Publisher resigns them with his prostrate service whilst he breaths, and is W. M.' In other editions the success of the book calls on the author to give it 'a new birth', i.e. a new preface. W. M., when age will not suffer him 'to remain much longer in this troublesome world', claims to have transcribed these receipts into the Queen's own book.

'The Pearle of Practice' is medical, and equals, if it does not exceed, any of its predecessors. For 'a special water for a consumption' there are used a peck of snails, a quart of earthworms, and three gallons of strong ale. 'The soiling of a Dog that is hard and white, mixed with honey' is recommended as an outward application to the throat. Superfluous hairs are removed by 'Cats dung that is hard and dryed, beaten to powder, and tempered with strong Vinegar'. The recipe for 'The Lady Gorings water for any Ague Sicknesse or foulenesse in the Stomach, and to purge the Blood' is, 'Take the Dung of a Stone-Horse that is kept in the stable when it is new made, mingle it well with Beer and a little Ginger, and a good quantity of Treacle, and distill it in an ordinary Still; Give of this a pretty draught to drink.'

'A Queens Delight' is 'The Art of Preserving, Conserving, and Candying', but also contains some medical recipes. It tells how 'To make a Cake the way of the Royal Princess, the Lady Elizabeth daughter to King Charles the first', and how to make 'Lorenoes' and 'an Ipswitch Ball'. A mysterious thing is 'A Receipt to make Damnable Hum', unless one knows that hum was a sort of strong ale, perhaps so named from the humming it caused in the head. A damnable hum must have been a drink of dangerous strength.

'The Compleat Cook' contains such interesting recipes as 'To make a Devonshire white-pot', 'To make a Outlandish dish' (hog's liver seasoned with aniseed), 'The Jacobins Pottage', 'To make a Battalia Pye', 'To make a Stumpe Pye', 'The Countesse of Rutlands Receipt of making the rare Banbury Cake, which was so much praised at her Daughters (the Lady Chaworths) wedding', 'To make a fat Lambe of a Pig', 'To make poor Knights'.

1655 HEALTHS IMPROVEMENT:

or, Rules Comprizing and Discovering the Nature, Method, and Manner of Preparing all sorts of food used in this nation. Written by that ever Famous Thomas Muffett, Doctor in Physick; Corrected and Enlarged by Christopher Bennett,

Doctor in Physick, and Fellow of the Colledg of Physicians in London.

London, printed by Tho. Newcomb for Samuel Thomson, at the sign of the White Horse in Pauls Churchyard, 1655.

This is a very interesting book on the choice and preparation of food by Thomas Muffett, who was born in 1553 and died in 1604. He became M.P. for Wilton in 1597. The book bears the imprimatur of the President and Censors of the College of Physicians. It was reprinted in 1746.

1656 THE PERFECT COOK.

Being the most exact directions for the making all kind of Pastes, with the perfect way teaching how to Raise, Season, and make all sorts of Pies, Pasties, Tarts, and Florentines, etc., now practised by the most famous and expert Cooks, both French and English.

As also the perfect English Cook, or right method of the whole Art of Cookery, with the true ordering of French, Spanish, and Italian Kickshaws, with Alamode varieties for Persons of Honour.

To which is added, the way of dressing all manner of Flesh, Fowl, and Fish, and making admirable Sauces, after the most refined way of French and English.

The like never extant;

With fifty-five ways of dressing of Eggs.

By Mounsieur Marnette.

Printed at London for Nath. Brooks at the Angel in Cornhil, 1656.

There is a frontispiece of two men and a woman in a kitchen, engraved by Ro. Vaughan. A later edition of 1686 has no frontispiece, and probably this edition did not have one.

From the preface we see that the author was born in London of foreign parents, and was 'turned young into the wild and Military World, to become a Son of Mars'. After a time he returned to London and resigned himself ' to Minerva's milder tuition and protection '. He apologizes for presenting a book on pastry ' to this Nation, where every Matron and young Damsel are so well vers'd

ENGLISH COOKERY BOOKS

in the Pastry Art, as that they may out-vie the best Forreign Pastry Cooks in all the World besides '

The book seems to be the one mentioned in London's Catalogue of the most vendible books (1657) as ' The French and English cooke, for exact making all sorts of pasts, pasties, Florentines, &c. ordering of French, Spanish, and Italian kickshawes, dressing, flesh, fowle, and fish ; with admirable sawces 12° '.

The first part of the book is a translation of *Le Pastissier françois*, which was published in 1653. An Amsterdam edition of 1655 has the same frontispiece as the English edition and the original of its preface. There are recipes for making Chossons, Flawns, Rattoones, Darioles, Poupelains, Tourrons, buttered Wiggs, Gamby Bisket, and the good Wives Tart or a Tart for a friend in a corner, all of which seem very good. The 55 ways of dressing eggs include ' an Omelet according to the newest mode, Oxford Gates, or the Covent Garden guise '.

1658 ARCHIMAGIRUS ANGLO-GALLICUS:

or, Excellent & approved Receipts and Experiments in Cookery

Together with the best way of Preserving.

As also, Rare Formes of Sugar-works :

According to the French Mode, and English Manner.

Copied from a choice Manuscript of Sir Theodore Mayerne Knight, Physician to the late K. Charles.

Magistro Artis, Edere est Esse.

Printed for G. Bedell, and T. Collins, and are to be sold at their shop at the Middle-Temple-Gate, in Fleet-street, 1658.

Sir Theodore Turquet de Mayerne was born at Mayerne, near Geneva, in 1573. He came to London in 1606, and was appointed physician first to the queen and then to the king. He died at Chelsea in 1655. Most, if not all, of the recipes are copied from earlier books. The compiler, who doubtless invented the fiction of a Mayerne manuscript, in a learned preface quotes Plato and Plautus.

1660 THE ACCOMPLISHT COOK,

Or the Art and Mystery of Cookery. Wherein the whole Art is revealed in a more easie and perfect Method, then hath been publisht in any Language, Expert and ready wayes for the Dressing of all sorts of Flesh, Fowl, and Fish ; the Raising of Pastes ; the best Directions for all manner of Kickshaws, and the most Poinant Sauces ; with the Tearms of Carving and Sewing. An exact Account of all Dishes for the Season ; with other a la mode Curiosities. Together with the lively Illustrations of such necessary Figures as are referred to Practice.

Approved by the Fifty Years Experience and Industry of Robert May, in his attendance on several Persons of Honour. London, printed by R. W. for Nath. Brooke, at the Sign of the Angel in Cornhill, 1660.

Other editions are 1665 (2), 1671 (3), of which there are two imprints, 1678 (4), 1685 (5).

As frontispiece there is a portrait with 'Æatis Suæ 71, 1660' in background, and beneath are the lines :

> What ! wouldst thou view but in one face
> all hospitalitie, the race
> of those that for the Gusto stand,
> whose tables a whole Ark comand
> of Nature's plentie, wouldst thou see
> this sight, peruse May's booke, tis hee.
> Ja. Parry

For Nathaniell Brooke, att the Angell in Cornehill.

According to Granger (Biog. Hist. iv. 68) the portrait is by Gaywood. Southey quotes the title-page in Omniana, ii. 70.

There are two poems at the beginning in May's honour, and a story of his life which mentions that he was the son of a cook and was trained in France. This training accounts for his giving nine recipes for preparing snails and one for baking frogs. In the preface May says that 'God and my own Conscience would not permit me to bury these my Experiences in the Grave', and that 'The Queens Closet Opened ' was the only book comparable to his own.

1661 THE WHOLE BODY OF COOKERY DISSECTED, Taught, and fully manifested, Methodically, Artificially, and according to the best Tradition of the English, French, Italian, Dutch, &c.

Or, a Sympathie of all varieties in Naturall Compounds in that Mysterie.

ENGLISH COOKERY BOOKS

Wherein is contained certain Bills of Fare for the Seasons of the year, for Feasts and Common Diets.

Whereunto is annexed a Second Part of Rare Receipts of Cookery; With certain useful Traditions.

With a Book of Preserving, Conserving and Candying, after the most Exquisite and Newest manner: Delectable for Ladies and Gentlewomen.

London, printed by R. W. for Giles Calvert, at the sign of the black Spread Eagle, at the West end of Pauls, 1661.

This book is by William Rabisha, who describes himself as 'Master Cook to many honourable Families before and since the wars began, both in this my Native Countrey, and with Embassadors and other Nobles in certain forraign patts'

Other editions are 1673, 1675 (2). Watt gives one of 1682. The editions of 1661 and 1673 are in the Bodleian, but not in the B. M.

There is a long poem in commendation of the author, two of the lines being:

> His Broths, Pottages, to the taste and sight,
> Would Esau-like, make some to sell their right.

It is a well-arranged book, giving recipes 'to pickle Sleep-at-noon', to make 'Punnado' and 'Andolians', 'to fry Primrose-leaves in March with eggs', 'to Spitchcoch an Eel'. Near the end are 'Certain old useful Traditions of Carving and Sewing, &c.' which come from the 'Book of Carving' of 1508, and a dreadful recipe 'to roast a shoulder of Mutton in blood'.

1661 THE LADIES DIRECTORY,

In Choice Experiments & Curiosities of Preserving and Candying both Fruits & Flowers. Also an Excellent way of making Cakes and other Comfits: With Rarities of many Precious Waters (among which are several Consumption Drinks, Approved of by the Doctors) and Perfumes. By Hanna Woolley, who hath had the Honour to perform such things the Entertainment of His late Majesty, as well as for the Nobility.

To prevent Counterfeits: Take Notice, that these books are no where to be had, but from the Authress, and at Peter Drings at the Sun in the Poultery, Book-seller;

and at Tho. Milbourns, Printer, in Jewen street near Aldersgate-Street: Who also sells for her, a most excellent Cordial-Powder, and very soveraign Pils,

London, printed by Tho. Milbourn for the Authress 1661.

There is another edition of 1662, which has a frontispiece representing a lady and her cook in a kitchen.

This is the first book by this authoress, who, according to the D. N. B., was married at the age of 24 to one Woolley, who had been master of the free school at Newport, and was married in 1666 to a Francis Challinor, of St. Margaret's, Westminster. Granger (Biog. Hist. v. 308) expresses doubt as to the real authorship of the books ascribed to her. In the preface she speaks of 'this little Book, which though but little, containeth more than all the books that ever I saw Printed in this Nature, they being rather Confounders than Instructers'.

1663 A BOOK OF KNOWLEDGE

In three parts, &c., &c.

Composed by Samuel Strangehopes.

London, printed for Charles Tyns, at the three Bibles on London-Bridge, 1663.

This book, of which there were several editions, contains a few recipes.

1664 THE COOKS GUIDE:

or, Rare Receipts for Cookery. Published and set forth particularly for Ladies and Gentlewomen; being very beneficial for all those that desire the true way of dressing of all sorts of Flesh, Fowles, and Fish; the best Directions for all manner of Kickshaws, and the most Ho-good Sawces: Whereby Noble Persons and others in their Hospitalities may be gratified in their Gusto's. Never before Printed.

By Hannah Wolley.

London, printed for Peter Dring at the Sun in the Poultry, next door to the Rose-Tavern, 1664.

The authoress says in her preface, 'I would not willingly dye while I live, nor be quite forgotten when I am dead; therefore have I sent forth This book, to testifie to the scandalous World that I do not altogether spend my Time idlely.'

1664 THE COURT & KITCHIN
of Elizabeth, Commonly called Joan Cromwel, The Wife of the late Usurper, Truly Described and Represented, And now made Publick for General Satisfaction.
London, printed by Tho. Milbourn, for Randal Taylor in St. Martins Le Grand, 1664.

A manuscript note in the B. M. copy says there should be a print as frontispiece. The paging and the lettering of the sheets are both irregular.

A long and learned introduction, quoting Epictetus and Plato, is an attack on the family of Cromwell, but its object must have been to act as an advertisement of the book, which is nothing but an ordinary cookery book. The recipes are introduced by this preface, ' Here followes the most usual Meat and Diet observed at her Table, most of them ordinary and vulgar, except some few Rarities, but such as arrided her Palate and Expense, of which it will be no unpleasing Labour to the Reader, to peruse the Cookery, and manner of Dressing, as also her Preserves, &c.' Two recipes have a definite personal reference attached, ' How to make Scotch Collops of Veal (this was almost her constant Dish)', ' How to make Marrow Puddings (which she usually had to her Breakfast)'.

(1664) THE GENTLEWOMANS CABINET UNLOCKED,
Wherein is contained many excellent Receipts for neat Dressing of divers sorts of Meats ; as Flesh and Fish, with their Proper Sauces. Also Directions for the best way of making

    Pancakes   Puddings   And such
    Fritters   Custards   like fine
    Tansies   Cheesecakes   Knacks.

And other Delicate Dishes, which are most frequently used in Gentlemens Houses.
Printed for W. Thackeray and T. Passenger.

Passenger succeeded to the business of Charles Tyas, his former master in 1664. Thackeray was in business in 1666.

The seventh edition was 1675, and the eighth was 1673, probably a misprint for 1678.

This is a small 8°, A to B₄, merely a compilation of a few recipes from previous books.

1668 CHOICE AND EXPERIMENTED RECEIPTS

in Physick and Chirurgery, as also Cordial and Distilled Waters and Spirits, Perfumes, and other Curiosities,

Collected by the Honourable and truly learned Sir Kenelm Digby, Kt., Chancellour to Her Majesty the Queen Mother. Translated out of several Languages, by G. H.

London, printed for the Author, and are to be sold by H. Brome, at the Star in Litte Britain, 1668.

The second edition was 1675. Sir Kenelm Digby was born in 1603 and died in 1665. He was one of the first fellows of the Royal Society, but seems to have been something of a mountebank, as Evelyn termed him. George Hartman was his steward according to Arber's Term Catalogues, ii. 16.

There is a portrait by Cross as frontispiece. This book is mainly medical and contains recipes, some of which are even more filthy and superstitious than those of any preceding books. 'A Sympathetick cure of the Tooth-ach. With an Iron-nail raise and cut the gum from about the Teeth, till it bleed, and that some of the blood stick upon the nail; then drive it into a woodden beam up to the head: After this is done, you never shall have the tooth-ach in all your life.'

1669 THE CLOSET OF THE EMINENTLY LEARNED SIR KENELME DIGBY, KT., OPENED:

Whereby is Discovered several Ways for making of Metheglin, Sider, Cherry-Wine, together with Excellent Directions for Cookery, as also for Preserving, Conserving, Candying. Published by his Son's Consent.

London, printed by E. C. for H. Brome, at the Star in Little Britain, 1669.

There is a portrait of Digby as frontispiece in this edition and the one of 1671. It is doubtful if the third edition (1677) had it.

An edition catalogued in the Bodleian as 1699 has 1669 on its title-page, but the third figure looks as if it had been altered with a pen. The title-page is a little different from the one given above.

ENGLISH COOKERY BOOKS

The book was reprinted in 1910.

The peculiarity of the book is the number of recipes for making drinks. There are nearly fifty recipes for making meath, and as many for making metheglin, in addition to recipes for hydromel, stepony, bragot, strawberry wine, cock-ale, &c. There is a recipe for making tea with eggs, and a warning against leaving tea to stand too long. 'The water is to remain upon it no longer than whiles you can say the Miserere Psalm very leisurely.'

1670 THE QUEEN-LIKE CLOSET

or Rich Cabinet : Stored with all manner of Rare Receipts for Preserving, Candying and Cookery. Very Pleasant and Beneficial to all Ingenious Persons of the Female Sex.
By Hannah Wolley.
Printed for R. Lowndes at the White Lion in Duck-Lane near West-Smithfield, 1670.

Other editions are 1672 (2), 1675 (3), 1681 (4), 1684 (5).

There is a frontispiece with five views of kitchen, distillery, &c. The third, fourth, and fifth editions have a supplement or 'A little of everything', separately paged and dated respectively 1674, 1680, and 1684.

There is not much that is new in this book except a recipe 'To make Misers for children to eat in afternoons in Summer'. At the end are directions for servants. The supplement contains the autobiography of Mrs. Wolley, a letter-writer, &c.

1672 THE LADIES DELIGHT,

or, a Rich Closet of Choice Experiments & Curiosities, containing the Art of Preserving & Candying both Fruits and Flowers : Together with The Exact Cook, or The Art of Dressing all sorts of Flesh, Fowl, and Fish. By Hannah Woolley. To which is Added : The Ladies Physical Closet : or Excellent Receipts, and Rare Waters for Beautifying the Face and Body.
London, printed by E. Milbourn, for N. Crouch, in Exchange-Alley over against the Royall-Exchange in Cornhil, 1672.

This is a new edition in one volume of 'The Ladies Directory' and 'The Cooks Guide'. The frontispiece is the same as in the 1662 edition of 'The Ladies Directory'. There was a German translation of this book printed at Hamburg in 1674.

1673 THE GENTLEWOMANS COMPANION;
or, a guide to the Female Sex: containing Directions of Behaviour, in all Places, Companies, Relations, and Conditions, from their Childhood down to Old Age, viz., as,

- Children to Parents.
- Scholars to Governours.
- Single to Servants.
- Virgins to Suitors.
- Married to Husbands.
- Huswifes to the House.
- Mistresses to Servants.
- Mothers to Children.
- Widows to the World.
- Prudent to all.

With Letters and Discourses upon all Occasions.

Whereunto is added, a Guide for Cook-maids, Dairy-maids, Chamber-maids, and all others that go to Service.

The whole being an exact Rule for the Female Sex in General.

By Hannah Woolley.

London, printed by A. Maxwell for Dorman Newman at the Kings-Arms in the Poultry, 1673.

Other editions are 1675, 1682 (3).

There is a portrait of a lady by Faithorne with a coat of arms as frontispiece. According to authorities quoted by the D. N. B. the lady is one Sarah Gilly.

Less than a sixth part of the book is devoted to cookery recipes. The introduction gives an account of the life of the authoress. 'Before I was Fifteen I was intrusted to keep a little School, and was the sole Mistress thereof.'

The book was reprinted in 1711 under the title of THE COMPLEAT GENTLEWOMAN. To it was added 'The Way to get Wealth, shewing how a Man may live plentfully for Two pence a Day'. This is a miscellaneous supplement, the value of which may be calculated by the cure for the bite of a mad dog. 'Write in a piece of paper these words, *Rebus, Rubus, Epitepscum*; give it to the Party or Beast bitten, to eat, in Bread. This never fails.'

1674 THE HOUSEWIFES COMPANION,
and the Husbandmans Guide, or the new Art of Cookery; exactly shewing the best ways for dressing all manner of Fish and Flesh, &c., concluding with the best and rarest Experiments for Planting, Grafting, Gardening, and curing

of Diseases in all sorts of useful Cattel; in octavo, price stitcht 6d. Printed for Tho. Passenger at the Three Bibles on London-Bridge.

This title is copied from Clavel's Catalogue. I have not seen the book itself.

1674 THE ENGLISH AND FRENCH COOK,

Describing the best and newest ways of ordering and dressing all sorts of Flesh, Fish, and Fowl, whether boiled, baked, stewed, roasted, broiled, frigassied, fryed, souc'd, marrinated, or pickled; with their proper Sauces and Garnished: Together with all manner of the most approved Soops and Potages used, either in England or France.

By T. P., J. P., R. C., N. B., and several other approved Cooks of London and Westminster.

London, printed for Simon Miller at the Star, at the West-end of St. Paul's, 1674.

This must be the book denounced in the third edition of 'The French Cook'.

It appeared in 1694 under the new title 'THE COMPLEAT COOK'. According to Arber there was an edition called 'THE COMPLEAT ENGLISH AND FRENCH COOK' in 1690, but I have not found it yet.

It seems a good and very well-arranged book, although there is little that is new in it. To 'The Compleat Cook' is added 'A Pocket-Companion; containing Things Necessary to be Known, by all that Values their Health and Happiness'. This is a short supplement said to be 'collected from The Good Housewife made a Doctor, by Tho. Tryon'. It recommends 'Mum' as a good drink.

1675 THE ACCOMPLISH'D LADY'S DELIGHT

In Preserving, Physick, Beautifying, and Cookery.
Containing,

I. The Art of Preserving, and Candying Fruits and Flowers, and the making of all sorts of Conserves, Syrups, and Jellies.

II. The Physical Cabinet, or, Excellent Receipts in Physick and Chirurgery; Together with some Rare

38   ENGLISH COOKERY BOOKS

  Beautifying waters, to adorn and add Loveliness to
the Face and Body : And also some New and Excellent Secrets and Experiments in the Art of Angling.

III. The Compleat Cooks Guide, or, directions for dressing
all sorts of Flesh, Fowl, and Fish, both in the English
and French Mode, with all Sauces and Sallets, and the
making Pyes, Pasties, Tarts, and Custards, with the
Forms and Shapes of many of them.

London, printed for B. Harris, and are to be Sold at his
Shop, at the Stationers Arms in Swithins Rents by the
Royall Exchange, 1675.

 Other editions are 1677 (2), 1683 (3), 1684 (4), 1685 (5), 1686 (6), 1696 (7), 1719 (10).

 There is a portrait of a lady as frontispiece, with the lettering, 'London, printed for Benjamin Harris'; round a half-title are views of distillery, boudoir, and kitchen. In the body of the book are an angling scene, drawings of eight varieties of fish, and shapes of pastry. There are separate title-pages to Part II, to the Art of Angling, and to Part III.

 The preface is signed T. P., and the book is catalogued under this title in the B. M.

 In the 1686 and later editions the Art of Angling is replaced by directions for starching and washing.

 There is nothing new in the cookery recipes, and many of the medical ones are absolutely filthy.

 There was a pamphlet published under the same title about 1780. See p. 112.

1676 KITCHIN-PHYSICK :
By way of Dialogue betwixt

    Philanthropos, Physician,
    Eugenius,   Apothecary,
    Lazarus,   Patient.

With Rules and Directions, how to prevent Sickness, and
cure Diseases by Dyet, and such things as are daily sold
in the Market : as also, for the better enabling of Nurses,
and such as attend sick People, there being nothing as yet
extant (though much desired) of this Nature.

London, printed for the Author, and are to be sold by
T. Basset at the George near Clifford's Inne in Fleet-street,
1676.

There are rules for the use of food. The second part is ' A practical
and short Discourse of stoving and bathing '. There is a plate of
a portable bath, very like the present cabinets for vapour baths.
The preface is signed Thomas Cocke.

1677 THE PLAIN DEALING POULTERER: or,
A Poulterer's Shop Opened: With
All Sorts of Ware, and how to know the Young from the
Old, being Dead or Alive.
Also how to Feed and Fatten Fowl in a short time, with
other things necessary to be known.
Very useful for Gentlemen and others, that they may not
be Deceived.
By Adam Shewring, a Poulterer.

> If that thou intend well to fare,
> Be wise in Chusing Poulter's ware

London, printed by C. Brome, at the Gun at the West-end
of Saint Paul's, 1677.

This perhaps should not be included, but it is interesting from
a cook's point of view.

1677 THE COMPLEAT SERVANT-MAID;
or the Young Maidens Tutor.
Directing them how they may fit, and qualifie themselves
for any of these Employments, viz.,

> Waiting-Woman, House-keeper, Chamber-Maid, Cook-Maid, Under Cook-Maid, Nursery-Maid, Dairy-Maid, Laundry-Maid, House-Maid, Scullery-Maid.

Composed for the great benefit and advantage of all young
Maidens.

London, printed for T. Passinger, at the Three Bibles on London Bridge, 1677.

This must have been a useful little book as it gives directions for writing and arithmetic as well as cookery and medical recipes and general advice to servants. There are two engraved plates of handwriting opposite page 20.

Hazlitt gives the fifth edition as 1691.

The eighth edition was 1711. It has a short supplement. The two plates are omitted.

A ninth edition (1729) has a slightly different title-page and other small alterations, which give it the appearance of a counterfeit edition.

1678 RARE AND EXCELLENT RECEIPTS,
Experienced and Taught by Mrs. Mary Tillinghast, and now Printed for the Use of her Scholars only.

London, printed in the year 1678.

A little book of 30 pages. There was a second edition in 1690.

1681 THE TRUE WAY OF PRESERVING AND CANDYING.
And Making Several Sorts of Sweet-meats, According to the Best and Truest Manner.

Made Publick for the Benefit of all English Ladies and Gentlewomen; especially for my Scholars.

London, printed for the Author, in the Year, M DC LXXXI.

The book was reprinted in 1695.

1681 A NEW DIGESTER,
or Engine for softening Bones, containing the Description of its Make and Use in these Particulars, viz.,

Cookery, Voyages at Sea, Confectionary, Making of Drinks, Chymistry, and Dying.

With an Account of the Price a good big Engine will cost, and of the Profit it will afford.

By Denys Papin, M.D., Fellow of the Royal Society.

London, printed by J. M. for Henry Bonwicke at the Red Lyon in S. Paul's Church-yard, 1681.

A CONTINUATION OF THE NEW DIGESTER OF BONES.

Its improvements and new uses it hath been applyed to, both for Sea and Land.

Together with some Improvements and new Uses of the Air-Pump, tryed both in England and in Italy.

By Denis Papin, M.D., Fellow of the Royal Society.

London, printed by Joseph Streater, near Pauls-Wharf in Thames-street, and are to be sold by the Book-Sellers in London, 1687.

These books have the imprimatur of the Council of the Royal Society. Evelyn once had a dinner prepared by this engine, *vide* Diary, iii. 82, 83. Papin was born at Blois in 1647. He came to London and worked with Boyle. He died at Marbury in 1714.

1682 THE TRUE PRESERVER AND RESTORER OF HEALTH:

Being a Choice Collection of Select and Experienced Remedies for all Distempers incident to Men, Women, and Children. Selected from, and Experienced by the most Famous Physicians and Chyrurgeons of Europe.

Together with Excellent Directions for Cookery; as also for Preserving, and Conserving, and making all sorts of Metheglin, Sider, Cherry-Wine, &c.

With the Description of an Ingenious and Useful Engin for Dressing of Meat, and for Distilling the Choicest Cordial Waters without Wood, Coals, Candle, or Oyl.

Published for the Publick-good by G. Hartman, Chymist.

London, printed by T. B., and are to be sold at his House in Hewes-Court in Black-Friers, 1682.

This is by the author of 'Choice and Experimented Receipts'. The larger portion of the book is medical, some of the recipes being filthy. There is a diagram of the engine. A large number of the cookery recipes have personal names attached, e.g. 'My Lady of Monmouth Boyleth a Capon with White-Broath thus', 'Mrs. Stockdel's excellent small Cakes, which are much esteemed at Court, the

King himself hath eat of them ', 'My Lady Diana Peters her Scotch Collops '.

The second edition is 1684. There is another second edition which has a different title-page. It begins, ' Hartman's Curiosities of Art and Nature, or, The true preserver and restorer of health, &c., &c.,' and professes to give receipts for destroying buggs and rats, and for many other things, which are not in the book. It was ' printed by A. C. at the Ring in Little Britain, pr. 3s. Where is sold A thousand Notable Things to prevent the Plague and all Distempers ; The Way to get Wealth and The Way to save Wealth '.

1682 A PERFECT SCHOOL OF INSTRUCTIONS FOR THE OFFICERS OF THE MOUTH :

Shewing the whole Art of

<table>
<tr><td>A Master of the Household
A Master Carver
A Master Butler</td><td>A Master Confectioner
A Master Cook
A Master Pastryman</td></tr>
</table>

Being a Work of singular Use for Ladies and Gentlewomen, and all Persons whatsoever that are desirous to be acquainted with the most Excellent Arts of Carving, Cookery, Pastry, Preserving, and Laying a Cloth for Grand Entertainments. The like never before extant in any Language.

Adorned with Pictures curiously Ingraven, displaying the whole Arts.

By Giles Rose, one of the Master Cooks in His Majesties Kitchen.

London, printed for R. Bentley and M. Magnes, in Russel-street, in Covent-Garden, 1682.

This is a translation of *L'escole parfaite des officiers de Bouche*, which was published at Paris in 1662.

It seems an excellent book, although it contains some strange things : ' Wine for the Gods ', ' Sauce d'Enfer ', ' Sheeps Feet for an Afternoon drinking '. There are directions for carving and for folding napkins. There are dozens of ways of cooking eggs—' eggs a l'Intrigue ', ' eggs a la Negligence ', &c.—and dozens of different pies and tarts, including ' a tart of frogs ' and ' a tart made with a tortoise '.

ENGLISH COOKERY BOOKS

1682-1702 There are some books written by Thomas Tryon, either in his own name or under the pseudonym 'Phylotheus Physiologus', which relate to food and diet and advocate vegetarianism. They are

HEALTHS GRAND PRESERVATIVE. 1682.

A TREATISE OF CLEANNESS IN MEATS AND DRINKS. 1682.

THE WAY TO HEALTH, LONG LIFE AND HAPPINESS. 1683, 1691(2), 1697(3).

THE WAY TO MAKE ALL PEOPLE RICH. 1685.

MISCELLANIA. 1696.

MONTHLY OBSERVATIONS. 1688.

WISDOMS DICTATES. 1691.

THE GOOD HOUSE-WIFE MADE A DOCTOR. N.D.(1), 1692(2).

THE WAY TO SAVE WEALTH OR NOTABLE THINGS. N.D.(1), 1697(2).

THE WAY TO GET WEALTH. 1702, 1706(2).

1683 THE YOUNG COOKS MONITOR:

or Directions for Cookery and Distilling, Being a choice Compendium of Excellent Receipts, made Publick for the Use and Benefit of my Schollars. By M. H.

London, printed by William Downing in Great St. Bartholomew-Close, 1683.

The second edition, which has an appendix, is 1690. There is nothing new in the book.

1687 THE ACCOMPLISHED LADIES RICH CLOSET OF RARITIES:

Or, the Ingenious Gentlewoman and Servant-Maids Delightful Companion. Containing many Excellent Things for the Accomplishment of the Female Sex, after the exactest Manner and Method, viz.

(1) The Art of Distilling. (2) Making Artificial Wines. (3) Making Syrups. (4) Conserving, Preserving, &c. (5) Candying and Drying Fruits, &c. (6) Confectioning.

(7) Carving. (8) To make Beautifying waters, Oyls, Pomatums, Musk-balls, Perfumes, &c. (9) Physical and Chyrurgical Receipts. (10) The Duty of a Wet Nurse; and to know and cure Diseases in Children, &c. (11) The Compleat Chamber-Maids Instructions in Pickling, making Spoon-meats, Washing, Starching, taking out Spots and Stains, Scowring Gold or Silver-Lace, Point, &c. (12) The Experienced Cook-Maid, or Instructions for Dressing, Garnishing, Making Sawces, serving up ; together, with the Art of Pastry. (13) Bills of Fare. (14) The Accomplished Dairy-Maids Directions, &c. (15) The Judicious Midwives Directions, how Women in Travail before and after Delivery ought to be used ; as also the Child ; and what relates to the Preservation of them both.

To which is added a Second Part, Containing Directions for the guidance of a Young Gentlewoman as to her Behaviour and seemly Deportment, &c.

The Second Edition, with many Additions.

London, printed by W. W. for Nicholas Boddington in Duck-Lane ; and Josiah Blare on London-Bridge, 1687.

The preface is signed John Shirley.

Other editions are 1691 (3), 169– (4), 1696 (5), 1699 (also 5).

There is a frontispiece representing a lady in her kitchen, garden, bedroom, &c.

This book has a wider range of subjects than preceding ones. There is a recipe ' To restore a ruby face to its former complexion ', and another 'To make a young face exceedingly beautiful, and an old face very tollerable '. There are fewer nasty recipes than in former books, but an old one for the Falling-Sickness is preserved, which consists of the powdered scull of a man ' that has not been above a year buried ', a nutmeg, and the blood of a dog, taken in white wine or new milk every morning and evening.

Much of the second part seems adapted from Mrs. Woolley's Gentlewomans Companion.

1693 THE GENTEEL HOUSE-KEEPERS PASTIME : Or, the Mode of Carving at the Table Represented in a Pack of Playing Cards.

ENGLISH COOKERY BOOKS 45

By which, together with the Instructions in this Book, any ordinary Capacity may easily learn how to Cut up or Carve in Mode all the most usual Dishes of Flesh, Fish, Fowl, and Baked Meats ; and how to make the several Services of the same at the Table ; with the several Sawces and Garnishes proper to each Dish of Meat.
Set forth by several of the best Masters in the Faculty of Carving, and Published for publick Use.
London, printed for J. Moxon, and sold at his Shop at the Atlas in Warwick-lane ; and at the three Bells in Ludgate-street, 1693.

This little duodecimo (A to C in eights, D with 4 leaves contains only advertisements) is in the Bodleian. The pack of cards is not with the book.

1695 THE FAMILY DICTIONARY ;
Or, Household Companion : Wherein are Alphabetically laid down Exact Rules and Choice Physical Receipts for the Preservation of Health, Prevention of Sickness, and Curing the several Diseases, Distempers, and Grievances, incident to Men, Women, and Children.
Also, Directions for Making Oils, Ointments, Salves, Cordial-Waters, Powders, Pills, Bolus's, Lozenges, Chymical Preparations, Physical Wines, Ales, and other Liquors, &c., and Descriptions of the Virtues of Herbs, Fruits, Flowers, Seeds, Roots, Barks, Minerals, and Parts of Living Creatures, used in Medicinal Potions, &c.
Likewise, Directions for Cookery in Dressing Flesh, Fish, Fowl, Seasoning, Garnishing, Sauces, and Serving-up in the Best and most acceptable Manner. The Whole Art of Pastry, Conserving, Preserving, Candying, Confectioning, &c.
Also the Way of Making all sorts of Perfumes, Beautifying-Waters, Pomatums, Washes, Sweet-Balls, Sweet-Bags, and Essences: Taking Spots and Stains out of Garments, Linnen,

&c., and Preserving them from Moths, &c. Washing Point, Sarsnets, and Restoring Faded Linnen ; and Scowring, or Brightening Tarnished Gold or Silver Lace, Plate, &c. Together, with the Art of Making all sorts of English Wines, as Currants, Cherries, Gooseberries, and Cyder, Mead, Metheglin, &c. And the Arts of Fining and Recovering Foul or Faded Wines. The Mystery of Pickling, and keeping all sorts of Pickles throughout the Year.

To which is added as an Appendix, the Explanation of Physical Terms, Bills of Fare in all Seasons of the Year. With the Art of Carving and many other Useful Matters.

By J. H.

London, printed for H. Rhodes, at the Star, the Corner of Bride-lane, in Fleet-street, 1695.

The second edition was published in 1696 with a new preface and the name of William Salmon, the quack doctor, as author, and with no mention of J. H. Other editions were 1705 (3) and 1710 (4).

The book is a mixture of cookery and medicine arranged alphabetically.

1699 ACETARIA. A DISCOURSE OF SALLETS,
By J. E., S.R.S., Author of the Kalendarium.

Οὐ παντὸς ἀνδρὸς ἔστιν ἀρτῦσαι καλῶς.

Crat. in Glauc.

London, Printed for B. Tooke, at the Middle-Temple Gate in Fleetstreet, 1699.

By John Evelyn. There is a folding plate between pages 108 and 109. The second edition was 1706. There is a modern reprint. The recipes are in the appendix. The quotation is abbreviated from the Glaucos of Cratinus, ' It is in every man's power to season well '.

1701 THE WHOLE DUTY OF A WOMAN:
or a Guide to the Female Sex, from the Age of Sixteen to Sixty, &c. Being Directions, How Women of all Qualities and Conditions, ought to Behave themselves in the various

Circumstances of this Life, for their Obtaining not only Present, but Future Happiness.

I. Directions how to Obtain the Divine and Moral Vertues of Piety, Meekness, Modesty, Chastity, Humility, Compassion, Temperance and Affability, with their Advantages, and how to avoid the Opposite Vices.

II. The Duty of Virgins, Directing them what they ought to do, and what to avoid for gaining all the Accomplishments required in that State. With the Whole Art of Love, &c. 3. The Whole Duty of a Wife. 4. The Whole Duty of Widow, &c. Also Choice Receipts in Physick, and Chirurgery. With the Whole Art of Cookery, Preserving, Candying, Beautifying, &c.

Written by a Lady.

The Third Edition.

London, Printed for J. Guillim, against the great James Tavern in Bishopgate-street. 1701.

Other editions are 1707 (4), 1712 (5), 1735 (8). To the latter is a frontispiece representing above a girl praying and below a girl cooking.

As we shall see later, a book dated 1737, also called 'The whole Duty of a Woman', is a different work. Another book with the same title, of which there were several American editions, is again different and treats only of religious subjects.

1702 THE COURT AND COUNTRY COOK:
giving New and Plain Directions How to Order all manner of Entertainments, And the best sort of the most exquisite a-la-mode Ragoo's. Together with New Instructions for Confectioners: Shewing

How to Preserve all sorts of Fruits, as well dry as liquid: Also,

How to make divers Sugar-works, and other fine pieces of Curiosity;

How to set out a Desert, or Banquet of Sweet-Meals to the best advantage ; And,

How to Prepare several sorts of Liquors, that are proper for every Season of the Year.

A Work more especially necessary for Stewards, Clerks of the Kitchen, Confectioners, Butlers, and other Officers, and also of great use in private Families.

Faithfully translated out of French into English by J. K.

London, Printed by W. Onley, for A. and J. Churchill at the Black Swan in Pater-noster-row, and M. Gillyflower in Westminster-hall, 1702.

This is a translation of *Le Cuisinier roial et bourgeois* by Massialot, which was published in 1691, and of *Nouvelle instruction pour les confitures, les liqueurs, et les fruits*, published in 1692. The latter book is also by Massialot, although Vicaire does not ascribe it to him.

It seems an excellent book and is provided with copious indices and glossaries. The cookery portion is arranged in alphabetical order.

1704 A TREATISE OF FOODS IN GENERAL :

First, The Difference and Choice which ought to be made of each sort in particular.

Secondly, The Good and Ill Effects produced by them.

Thirdly, The Principles wherewith they abound. And,

Fourthly, The Time, Age and Constitution they suit with. To which are added,

Remarks upon each Chapter ; wherein their Nature and Uses are explained, according to the Principles of Chymistry and Mechanism.

Written in French, by M. Louis Lemery, Regent-Doctor of the Faculty of Physick at Paris, and of the Academy Royal of Sciences. Now done into English.

London, printed for John Taylor, at the Ship in St. Paul's-Church-yard. M DCC IV.

To this book is appended the imprimatur of the College of Physicians, as well as translations of those given by the University of Paris and the Royal Academy of Sciences.

The translation is by D. Hay, M.D.

Louis Lemery, doctor and chemist, the brilliant son of a distinguished Paris doctor, lived from 1677 to 1743. This was his first book.

There were two imprints in MDCCXLV. One, called the third edition, has a frontispiece representing five men with the lines underneath:

> Charles and his merry Courtiers here you see
> Sporting with wit, and Jest, and Repartee.

It is a very interesting book and full of ancient lore and superstition.

1705 APICII COELII DE OPSONIIS ET CONDIMENTIS,

Sive Arte Coquinaria, Libri Decem. Cum Annotationibus Martini Lister, è Medicis domesticis serenissimae Majestatis Reginae Annae.

Et Notis selectioribus, variisque lectionibus integris, Humelbergii, Caspari Barthii, & Variorum.

Londini, Typis Gulelmi Bowyer. MDCCV.

Only 120 copies were printed. A second edition, limited to 100 copies, was published at Amsterdam in 1709. The publication of this book by Martin Lister, the most distinguished physician of the day, gave rise to a satirical poem called 'The Art of Cookery'.

1705 THE PASTRY-COOKS VADE-MECUM:

or a Pocket-Companion for Cooks, House-keepers, Country Gentlewomen, &c., Containing, Choice and Excellent Directions, and Receipts for making all Sorts of Pastry-Work; Dressing the most Dainty Dishes; Candying, Preserving, and Dying all manner of Fruit. As also, the Art of Distilling and Surgery.

London, printed for Abel Roper, at the Black-Boy in Fleet-street, 1705.

There are some pleasant recipes, 'Syrup of Peach Blossoms,' and 'To make an excellent Liquor called Shrub', but the medical recipes are not all so nice. For 'A Cordial Jelly for the Recovery from the Rickets', one must 'take a red Cock with yellow Legs, and smother him to death'. 'The cold snail water' contains 100 snails and 'a Pint of great Earth worms' boiled in a gallon of new milk 'of a Red Cow'.

ENGLISH COOKERY BOOKS

1705 BEAUTIES TREASURY:
or, The Ladies Vade Mecum, being a Collection of the Newest, most Select and Valuable Receipts, for making all Sorts of Cosmetick-Washes, Oils, Unguents, Waters, &c. Useful in Repairing lost Beauty, maintaining and improving good Complections, removing Blemishes of any kind, and procuring Handsomness. To which are added, Receipts for making the best Cordial-Waters, as also the Finest Essences, and especially a Collection of the best Perfumes, and excellent Snuffs. Published for the General Good, after many Years Experience of the Efficacy and Excellence of every one of them. By J. W. . . . Philo-Chym & Med. London, printed and to be sold, by S. Malthus next the Rose and Crown in London House-Yard, near the West-end of St. Paul's: 1705.
Price Bound One Shilling.

<small>There are a few cookery recipes, but most of the book corresponds to its title.</small>

1706 THE HOUSE-KEEPERS GUIDE,
in the Prudent Managing of Their Affairs, being several Observations relating to the Orderly and Discreet Government of Private Families, Grounded upon Reason, Experience, and the Word of God. Recommended to all Young House-keepers, for their Benefit and Advantage.

> Non minus est Virtus quam quaerere, parta tueri,
>   Casus inest illic, hoc erit Artis opus.
> OVID.
> Dî sibi Divitias dederant, artemque fruendi.
> HOR. *Epist.* 1, 2.

London, printed for A. Bosvile at the Dial and Bible against St. Dunstans Church in Fleetstreet. 1706.

<small>A figure of Prudence is the frontispiece, and the preface is signed C. R. The headline is 'The Young House-keepers Guide'. The book is purely devotional, and is entered here as a warning to</small>

collectors who may see the title in a catalogue. An extract from
'A Servants Prayer' may be of interest. 'I humbly submit to the
State wherein Thou hast been pleased to place me, below many
others, in the low Condition of a Servant ; and as my Talents are
few, so at the day of Judgment my Accompt shall be less. . . .
Help me to demean myself so humbly, and whatsoever I do to do
it so heartily, that I may obtain Favour in their Eyes. Or if they
be froward and hard to please, O God preserve me from all unseeming
Passions, and disrespectful Behaviour towards them.'

1708 ENGLANDS NEWEST WAY

in all sorts of cookery, pastry, and all pickles that are fit
to be used. Adorn'd with Copper Plates, setting forth the
Manner of placing Dishes upon Tables ; and the Newest
Fashions of Mince-Pies. By Henry Howard, Free-Cook of
London, and late Cook to his Grace the Duke of Ormond,
and since to the Earl of Salisbury, and Earl of Winchelsea.
Likewise the best Receipts for making Cakes, Mackroons,
Biskets, Ginger-bread, French-bread : As also for Preserving, Conserving, Candying and Drying Fruits, Confectioning
and making of Creams, Syllabubs, and Marmalades of
several sorts.

The Second Edition with Additions and Amendments.

London, printed for and sold by Chr. Coningsby, at the
Ink-bottle against Clifford's-Inn Back-Gate, in Fetter-lane,
Fleetstreet. 1708.

Other editions are 1710 (3) and 1726 (5). Mrs. Pennell gives the
first edition as 1703. There are recipes for making a Hogooe,
a Monastick, a Dowlett Pye, and a Tart de May.

1708 THE ART OF COOKERY :

a poem in imitation of Horace's art of poetry.

This is the poem which satirizes Martin Lister's edition of Apicius
Coelius. It is by W. King.

1709 THE QUEEN'S ROYAL COOKERY :

or, Expert and ready Way for the Dressing of all Sorts of
Flesh, Fowl, Fish : Either Bak'd, Boil'd, Roasted, Stew'd,

Fry'd, Broil'd, Hash'd, Frigasied, Carbonaded, Forc'd, Collar'd, Sous'd, Dry'd, &c. After the Best and Newest Way. With their several Sauses and Salads. And making all sorts of Pickles. Also Making Variety of Pies, Pasties, Tarts, Cheese-Cakes, Custards, Creams, &c. With the Art of Preserving and Candying of Fruits and Flowers ; and the making of Conserves, Syrups, Jellies, and Cordial Waters. Also making several Sorts of English Wines, Cyder, Mead, Metheglin. Together, with several Cosmetick or Beautifying Waters : And also several sorts of Essences and Sweet Waters, by Persons of the highest Quality. By T. Hall, Free-Cook of London.

The Second Edition.

London, printed for C. Bates, at the Sun and Bible in Giltspur-street, in Pye-corner : And A. Bettesworth, at the Red Lion on London-Bridge, 1713.

Licensed according to Order.

The first edition was 1709, but I omitted to note the title-page when I saw the book. Other editions are 1719 (3) and 1730 (5).

There is a frontispiece with a portrait of Queen Anne, and representations of a kitchen, &c.

The preface states that the book ' has a singular Advantage over most Books of this kind. . . . It is not stuff'd with superfluous Trifles, as most of its Nature are; or with old and antiquated Receipts ; but with Things wholly new and useful '. In spite of this, however, most of the recipes seem copied from preceding works.

1710 ROYAL COOKERY ;

or, the Complete Court-Cook. Containing the Choicest Receipts in all the particular Branches of Cookery, now in Use in the Queen's Palaces of

  St. James's }   { Hampton-Court, and
  Kensington }   { Windsor.

With near Forty Figures (curiously engraven on Copper) of the magnificent Entertainments at Coronations, Instalment, Balls, Weddings, &c., at Court ; Also Receipts for

making the Soupes, Jellies, Bisques, Ragoo's, Pattys, Tanzies, Forc'd-Meats, Cakes, Puddings, &c.
By Patrick Lamb, Esq.; near 50 Years Master-Cook to their late Majesties King Charles ii, King James ii, King William and Queen Mary, and to Her Present Majesty Queen Anne.
To which are added, Bills of Fare for every Season in the Year.
London, printed for Abel Roper, and sold by John Morphew, near Stationers-Hall, 1710.

Other editions are 1716 (2), 1726 (3), 1731.

There is a half-title, 'Lamb's Royal Cookery.' The preface says, 'As for the Author of these Sheets, his Name and Character are so well known and establish'd in all the Courts of Christendom, that I need observe no more of him, than that he liv'd and dy'd a very great Rarity, having maintained his Station at Court, and the Favour of his Prince, for about Fifty Years together; which whoever does after him, may boast of being one of the Two fortunate and long-liv'd Courtiers, which perhaps an Hundred Ages before have not produc'd.'

1711 NEW CURIOSITIES IN ART AND NATURE:
or, A Collection of the most Valuable Secrets in all Arts and Sciences, as appears by the Contents. Being very Useful for all Persons who are desirous to consult their Health, Pleasure, or Beauty; enrich'd with an Infinite Variety of Curious Rarities in Perfuming, Colouring, Painting, making of Cordial Waters, Pomatums, Washes, Scenting of Snuffs and all Sort of Varieties of that Nature, which have been Try'd and Approv'd by People of the Best Quality.
Composed and Experimented by the Sieur Lemery, Apothecary to the French King.
Translated into English from the Seventh Edition, Printed this last Year in French, in which is near one half more than in any former Edition. Illustrated with Cuts. To which is added a Supplement by the Translator.
London, printed for John King at the Bible and Crown in

Little Britan, and sold by John Morphew, near Stationers Hall. 1711.

The book is by Nicolas, father of Louis Lemery. There are a few recipes in chapter xii.

1714 A COLLECTION OF ABOVE THREE HUNDRED RECEIPTS

in Cookery, Physick and Surgery; for the Use of all Good Wives, Tender Mothers, and Careful Nurses. By several Hands.

London, printed for Richard Wilkind, at the King's Head in St. Paul's Church-yard. M DCC XIV.

Other editions are 1719 (2), 1724 (3 and in some copies 2), 1728 (4), 1734 (5), 1746 (6), 1759 (7).

The book is by Mary Kittelby, who died between 1724 and 1734. There is a half-title, 'A Collection of Receipts in Cookery, Physick and Surgery.' A second part is added to the second and following editions.

There are recipes to make ' Thin Cream Pan-cakes, call'd a Quire of Paper ', ' Panada, for a Sick or Weak Stomach ', ' Salop ', ' London-wigs ', ' Birch-Wine, as made in Sussex '.

The authoress recommends her book to the clergy, ' especially to those whose Parishes are remote from other Help,' and her recipes, with the exception of three for snail water, seem admirably fitted for domestic use. What could be better ' To Help a Hot and Costive Habit of Body ' than this ? ' Roasted Apples with Carraway Comfits, eaten constantly every Night, has been the Method of a Gentleman of Fourscore, who has hardly ever taken other Physick, or omitted this for Fifty Years, and never felt the Gout, or Stone, or any other Distemper incident to Old Age.'

1717 DICTIONARIUM RUSTICUM, URBANICUM, & BOTANICUM:

or, A Dictionary of Husbandry, Gardening, Trade, Commerce, and all Sorts of Country-Affairs.

The Second Edition.

London, printed for J. Nicholson in Little Britain, W. Taylor in Ave-mary-Lane, and W. Churchill at the Black-Swan in Pater-noster-Row. 1717.

ENGLISH COOKERY BOOKS

The full title-page is not given as there are very few articles on cookery, and these are very brief. The book has been attributed to N. Bailey.

1718 MRS MARY EALES'S RECEIPTS.

Confectioner to her late Majesty Queen Anne.

London, printed by H. Meere in Black-Fryers, and to be had at Mr. Cooper's at the Three Pidgeons the lower End of Bedford-Street, near the New Exchange in the Strand. M DC XVIII.

This is a little book of 100 pages with no preface. It was reprinted twice in M DCC XXXIII. One of the reprints is called ' The Compleat Confectioner : or the Art of Candying and Preserving in its utmost Perfection. Being a Collection of all the Receipts of the late ingenious Mrs. Eales, Confectioner to their late Majesties King William and Queen Anne '. A second edition, ' corrected, with additions,' was M DCC LXVII. There was a fifth edition of ' The Compleat Confectioner ' reprint in 1753.

1723 COURT COOKERY :

or, The Compleat English Cook. Containing the Choicest and Newest Receipts for making Soops, Pottages, Fricasseys, Harshes, Farces, Ragoos, Cullises, Sauces, Forc'd-Meats and Souses ; with various Ways of Dressing most Sorts of Flesh, Fish and Fowl, Wild and Tame ; with the best Methods of Potting and Collaring. As Likewise of Pastes, Pies, Pastys, Pattys, Puddings, Tansies, Biskets, Creams, Cheesecakes, Florendines, Cakes, Jellies, Sillabubs and Custards. Also of Pickling, Candying and Preserving : With a Bill of Fare for every Month in the Year, and the latest Improvements in Cookery, &c.

By R. Smith, Cook (under Mr. Lamb) to King William ; as also to the Dukes of Buckingham, Ormond, D'Aumont (the French Ambassador) and others of the Nobility and Gentry. London, printed for T. Wotton, at the Three Daggers in Fleet Street. M DCC XXIII.

The author says in his preface, ' It is true, there are several Books of Cookery already extant, but most of 'em very defective and erroneous, and others filled with old Receipts, that are impracticable at this Time.' He denounces especially ' Royal Cookery ' to which the name of Lamb was attached and which contained recipes which were certainly not Lamb's.

The book is in two parts, and with a separate index. The first part consists of cookery; the second of pastry, confectionery, pickling, &c. In the latter part are recipes for ' A Sweet Chicken Pie ' and ' An excellent Carrot Pudding '.

1723 THE COOK'S AND CONFECTIONER'S DICTIONARY:

or, The Accomplish'd Housewife's Companion. Containing,
 I. The choicest Receipts in all the several Branches of Cookery; or the best and newest Ways of dressing all sorts of Flesh, Fish, Fowl, &c., for a Common or Noble Table; with their proper Garnitures and Sauces.
 II. The best way of making Bisks, Farces, forc'd Meats, Marinades, Olio's, Puptons, Ragoos, Sauces, Soops, Potages, &c., according to the English, French, and Italian Courts.
 III. All manner of Pastry-works, as Biskets, Cakes, Cheesecakes, Custards, Pastes, Patties, Puddings, Pyes, Tarts, &c.
 IV. The various Branches of Confectionary; as Candying, Conserving, Preserving, and Drying all sorts of Flowers, Fruits, Roots, &c. Also Jellies, Composts, Marmalades, and Sugar-works.
 V. The way of making all English potable Liquors; Ale, Beer, Cider, Mead, Metheglin, Mum, Perry, and all sorts of English Wines; Also Cordials, and Beautifying Waters.
 VI. Directions for ordering an Entertainment, or Bills of Fare for all Seasons of the Year; and setting out a Desert of Sweetmeats to the best Advantage: With an Explanation of the Terms us'd in Carving. According to the Practice of the most celebrated

Cooks, Confectioners, &c., in the Courts of England, France, &c., and of many private and accomplish'd Housewives.
Revised and Recommended by John Nott, Cook to his Grace the Duke of Bolton.
London, printed for C. Rivington, at the Bible and Crown, in St. Paul's Church-yard. M DCC XXIII.

Other editions are 1724 (2), 1726 (3), and 1733 (4). The book is arranged according to alphabetical order. There is a curious description at the beginning of the book of practical jokes which were played at banquets in old days.

1725 DICTIONAIRE OECONOMIQUE :
or, The Family Dictionary. Containing,
The most experienced Methods of improving Estates and of preserving Health, with many approved Remedies for most Distempers of the Body of Man, Cattle and other Creatures, and the best Means for attaining Long Life.
The most advantageous Ways of Breeding, Feeding, and Ordering all Sorts of Domestick Animals, as Horses, Kine, Sheep, Swine, Poultry, Bees, Silkworms, &c.
The different Kinds of Nets, Snares and Engines for taking all Sort of Fish, Birds, and other Game.
Great Variety of Rules, Directions, and new Discoveries, relating to Gardening, Husbandry, Soils and Manures of all Sorts ; the Planting and Culture of Vines, Fruit Trees, Forest Trees, Underwoods, Shrubs, Flowers, and their several Uses ; the Knowledge of Foreign Drugs, Dies, Domestick and Exotick Plants and Herbs, with their specifick Qualities and medicinal Virtues.
The best and cheapest Ways of providing and improving all Manner of Meats and Drinks ; of preparing several Sorts of Wines, Waters and Liquors for every Season, both by Distillation and otherwise :
Of preserving all kind of Fruits as well dry as liquid, and

making divers Sweetmeats and Works of Sugar, and other profitable Curiosities, both in the Confectionary and Culinary Arts of Housewifery.

Means of making the most Advantage of the Manufactures of Soap, Starch, Spinning, Cotton, Thread, &c.

The Methods to take or destroy Vermin and other Animals, injurious to Gardening, Husbandry, and all rural Œconomy; with a Description of Garden and other Country Tools and Utensils.

An Account of the several Weights, Measures, &c., of Metals and Minerals, with their Preparations and Uses.

All Sorts of Rural Sports and Exercises, conducing to the Benefit and innocent Enjoyments of Life ; as also Painting in Miniature, and divers other Arts and Terms of Art explained, for the Entertainment and Amusement of Gentlemen, Ladies, &c.

The whole illustrated throughout with very great Variety of Figures, for the readier understanding and practising of things to which they belong.

Done into English from the Second Edition, lately printed at Paris, in two Volumes, Folio, written by M. Chomel :
With considerable Alterations and Improvements.

Revised and Recommended by Mr. R. Bradley, Professor of Botany in the University of Cambridge, and F.R.S.
In Two Volumes.

London, printed for D. Midwinter, at the Three Crowns in St. Paul's Church-Yard. M DCC XXV.

The preface gives an account of Noel Chomel (1632–1712), who was a priest but had many relatives who were distinguished men of science.

1727 THE COUNTRY HOUSEWIFE AND LADY'S DIRECTOR,

in the Management of a House, and the Delights and Profits of a Farm. Containing

ENGLISH COOKERY BOOKS

Institutions for managing the Brew-House, and Malt-Liquors in the Cellar; the making of Wines of all sorts.

Directions for the Dairy, in the Improvement of Butter and Cheese upon the worst of Soils; the feeding and making of Brawn; the ordering of Fish, Fowl, Herbs, Roots, and all other useful Branches belonging to a Country Seat, in the most elegant manner for the Table.

Practical Observations concerning Distilling; with the best Method of making Ketchup, and many other curious and durable Sauces.

The Whole distributed in their proper Months, from the Beginning to the End of the Year.

With particular Remarks relating to the Drying or Kilning of Saffron.

By R. Bradley, Professor of Botany in the University of Cambridge, and F.R.S.

The Second Edition.

London, printed for Woodman, and Lyon, in Russell-street, Covent Garden. M DCC XXVII.

(Price 2s. 6d.)

There is a frontispiece representing a farm. The third edition is 1728. 'A sixth edition with additions' was published in 1732. It contains a second part, in which there is more cookery than in the first.

This same 'sixth edition with additions' was reprinted in 1736, the 1732 edition of the second part being bound with it.

The first part is arranged according to the months of the year. The second part has no order whatever, cures for lap-dogs being placed between recipes for making damson wine and Lisbon cakes. There is a recipe for a Hackin which Cumberland people have for breakfast on Christmas morning. 'And if this dish is not dressed by that time it is Day-light, the Maid is led through the Town, between two Men, as fast as they can run with her, up Hill and down Hill, which she accounts a great shame.' There are two dishes which are not likely to be imitated in the present day; one is a gammon of a badger roasted, the other is viper soup.

1727 THE COMPLEAT HOUSEWIFE ;
or, Accomplished Gentlewoman's Companion: being a Collection of upwards of Five Hundred of the most approved Receipts in

Cookery,	Cakes,
Pastry,	Creams,
Confectionary,	Jellies,
Preserving,	Made Wines,
Pickles,	Cordials.

With Copper Plates curiously engraven for the regular Disposition or Placing the various Dishes and Courses.
And also Bills of Fare for every Month of the Year.
To which is added, A Collection of near Two Hundred Family Receipts of Medicines ; viz. Drinks, Syrups, Salves, Ointments, and various other Things of soveraign and approved Efficacy in most Distempers, Pains, Aches, Wounds, Sores, &c., never before made publick ; fit either for private Families, or such publick-spirited Gentlewomen as would be beneficent to their poor Neighbours.
By E— S—
London, printed for J. Pemberton, at the Golden Buck, over-against St. Dunstan's Church in Fleet-street.
M DCC XXVII.

This book is by E. Smith and went through many editions ; 1728 (2), 1729 (3), 1730 (4), 1732 (5), 1734 (6), 1736 (7), 1737 (8), 1739 (9), 1741 (10), 1742 (11), 1744 (12), 1750 (14), 1753 (15), 1758 (16), 1766 (17), 1773 (18).

On the title-page to the fifth edition it is mentioned that 'near Fifty Receipts' were 'communicated just before the Author's Death '.

There is a frontispiece of a kitchen in some of the later editions.

The preface treats of cookery from the earliest times, and propounds difficult theological problems : 'That Esau was the first Cook, I shall not presume to assert ; for Abraham gave Order to dress a fatted Calf ; but Esau is the first Person mentioned that made any Advances beyond plain Dressing, as Boiling, Roasting, &c. For tho' we find indeed that Rebeckah his Mother was accomplished with the Skill of making savoury Meat as well as he, yet whether he learned it from her, or she from him, is a Question too knotty for me to determine.'

There are some curious recipes. 'Asparagus soop' is made of twelve pounds of lean beef, a quarter of a pound of butter, a pint of brown ale, half a hundred of asparagus, besides vermicelli, celery, and spinage. 'To mumble rabbets and chickens.' 'To make a Poloe.' 'To make a Pulpatoon of Pigeons.' 'To make a Tureiner.' The medical recipes are often very nasty, and the complaints sometimes are of such a nature that one would hardly expect the 'publick-spirited Gentlewomen' of the title-page to treat.

1730 THE COMPLETE PRACTICAL COOK:

or, A New System of the Whole Art and Mystery of Cookery.

Being a Select Collection of above Five Hundred Recipes for Dressing, after the most Curious and Elegant Manner (as well Foreign as English) all Kinds of Flesh, Fish, Fowl, &c.

As also Directions to make all Sorts of excellent Pottages and Soups, fine Pastry, both sweet and savoury, delicate Puddings, exquisite Sauces, and rich Jellies. With the best Rules for Preserving, Potting, Pickling, &c.

Fitted for all occasions : but more especially for the most Grand and Sumptuous Entertainments.

Adorned with Sixty Curious Copper Plates ; exhibiting the full Seasons of the Year, and Tables proper for Every Month ; as also Variety of large Ovals and Rounds, and Ambogues and Square Tables for Coronation-Feasts, Instalments, &c.

The Whole intirely New ; and none of the Recipes ever published in any Treatise of this Kind.

Approved by divers of the Prime Nobility ; and by several Masters of the Art and Mystery of Cookery.

By Charles Carter, Lately Cook to his Grace the Duke of Argyll, the Earl of Pontefract, the Lord Cornwallis, &c.

London, printed for W. Meadows, in Cornhill; C. Rivington

in St. Paul's Church-Yard; and R. Hett, in the Poultry. M DCC XXX.

<small>This is a large quarto with fine engravings of the courses at table. The preface speaks of 'the little low Arts used by Persons who have wanted to vamp up Old Books, and pass them upon the World for New, with the Name of a Modern Artist prefix'd, who has had no other Hand in the whole, than the extending of it to receive Five or Ten Guineas for the Credit of his Name'.</small>

1732 THE COMPLEAT CITY AND COUNTRY COOK; or, Accomplish'd Housewife. Containing Several Hundred of the most approv'd Receipts in

Cookery,	Pastry,
Confectionary,	Pickles,
Cordials,	Preserving,
Cosmeticks,	Syrups,
Jellies,	English Wines, &c.

Illustrated with Forty-nine large Copper Plates, directing the regular placing the various Dishes on the Table, from one to four or five Courses: Also, Bills of Fare according to the several Seasons for every Month of the Year.

Likewise, the Horse-shoe Table for the Ladies at the late Instalment at Windsor, the Lord Mayor's Table, and other Hall Dinners in the City of London; with a Fish Table, &c.

By Charles Carter, lately Cook to his Grace the Duke of Argyle, the Earl of Pontefract, the Lord Cornwallis, &c.

To which is added by way of Appendix, near Two Hundred of the most approv'd Receipts in Physick and Surgery for the Cure of the most common Diseases incident to Families: the Collection of a Noble Lady Deceased. A Work design'd for the Good, and absolutely Necessary for all Families.

London, printed for A. Bettesworth and C. Hitch; and C. Davis in Pater-noster Row: T. Green at

Charing-Cross ; and S. Austen in St. Paul's Church-yard. M DCC XXXII.

This is a smaller book than the last. The author in his preface says that his father was a cook before him. The recipes in the appendix once more show a horrid mixture of filth and superstition. 1736 (2).

1733 THE MODERN COOK,
by Mr. Vincent La Chapelle, Chief Cook to the Right Honourable the Earl of Chesterfield.
London, printed for the Author, and sold by Nicolas Prevost, at the Ship over-against Southampton-Street, in the Strand. M DCC XXXIII.

In two volumes. The second edition [1] (1736) is in three, the third (1744) and fourth (1751) in one. There are many plates of the courses at table.

This seems a most excellent and well-arranged book, though some of the recipes are strange. A 'strengthening broth' is made of two hundred sparrows with other ingredients. For besieged towns the author gives a recipe for 'broth cakes, which may be conveniently carried about, and preserv'd above a year'.

1733 THE HOUSE-KEEPER'S POCKET-BOOK,
and Compleat Family Cook. Containing above Three Hundred Curious and Uncommon Receipts in

Cookery,	Pickling,
Pastry,	Candying,
Preserving,	Collaring, &c.

With Plain and Easy Instructions for preparing and dressing everything suitable for an Elegant Entertainment, from Two Dishes to Five or Ten, &c. And Directions for placing them in their proper Order.
Concluding with many Excellent Prescriptions of the most Eminent Physicians, of singular Efficacy in most Distempers incident to the Human Body :
And to the whole is prefix'd, such a copious and useful Bill of Fare of all manner of Provisions in Season for every

[1]. This is also called the third in some copies.

Month of the Year, that no Person need be at a Loss to provide an agreeable Variety of Dishes.

By Mrs. Sarah Harrison of Devonshire.

London, printed for T. Worrall, at Judge Coke's Head, over against St. Dunstan's Church, Fleetstreet. 1733.

(Price 2s. 6d. bound.)

Other editions are 1739 (2), 1748 (4), 1751 (5), 1755 (6), 1757 (also 6), 1760 (7), 1764 (8), 1777 (9). A book with the same title was published in 1783, but is an entirely different work.

This book is neither original nor well arranged. Later editions are much enlarged and contain arithmetical tables and other additions. The medical receipts are expanded into a supplement called 'Every one their own Physician: or, Charity made pleasant, by relieving their own Family, or poor neighbouring People, by cheap, easy, and safe Remedies'. A preface to this supplement is signed 'Mary Morris'. The third recipe, one for ague, prejudices one at the start against Mary Morris. 'Take a Spider alive, cover it with new soft crummy Bread without bruising it; let the Patient swallow it fasting. This is an effectual Cure, but many are set against it.'

1734 FIVE HUNDRED NEW RECEIPTS

in

Cookery, Confectionary, Pastry, Preserving, Conserving, Pickling;

and the several Branches of these Arts necessary to be known by all good Housewives.

By John Middleton, Cook to his Grace the late Duke of Bolton.

Revised and Recommended by Mr. Henry Howard.

London, printed for Tho. Astley, at the Rose against the North Door of St. Paul's. MDCCXXXIV.

1734 THE YOUNG LADY'S COMPANION

in

Cookery, And Pastry, Preserving, Pickling, Candying, &c.

Containing the newest and best Receipts for making all Sorts of Broths, Gravies, Soups, Ragoo's, Hashes, &c. Dressing several Sorts of Meats, Collering, Potting, and making Force-Meats, &c.

Also making of Cakes, Creams, Jellies, Marmalades, Tarts, Puddings, Pies, Pasties, Biscuits, Custards, &c.

Likewise Preserving and Candying Angelico, Apples, Cherries, Currants, Figs, Goosberries, Grapes, Oranges, Peaches, Nectarines, &c.

Violets, Roses, Couslips, and other Flowers.

And the best Method of Pickling Melons, Cucumbers, Barberries, Mushrooms, Purflame, &c.

London, printed for A. Bettesworth and C. Hitch in Paternoster Row, J. Hazard against Stationers Hall, W. Bickerton and C. Corbett, without Temple-bar, and R. Willock, in Cornhill, 1734.

> A small book of recipes ' collected by a Gentlewoman who formerly kept a Boarding School '.

1735 THE GENTLEMAN'S COMPANION AND TRADESMAN'S DELIGHT.

Containing The Mystery of Dying in all its Branches. The Manner of preparing Colours. The Method of cleaning and taking out Stains from Silks, Woollen, or Linnen. To clean Gold or Silver Lace, and Plate. To prepare a Cement for China, or Glass.

The Art of Drawing, Limning, Painting, Etching, Engraving, Carving, Gilding, Enamelling, and Refreshing Pictures.

Likewise the Quality of Natural and Artificial Metals. How to harden or soften them. The Art of soldering, burnishing, and gilding Metals. To make all Sorts of Ink. To prepare Gold and Silver for Writing. To make Sealing-Wax, or Wafers. To know the Purity of Gold or Silver, and detect counterfeit Coins.

The great Mr. Boyle's Method of writing in such a Manner

as cannot be discovered without the help of Fire, Water, &c.
To take Blots out of Paper. The Art of dressing, cleaning, and perfuming Gloves and Ribbons, and washing all Sorts of Lace.

Also the Method of Curing and Preserving English Wines in the best Manner. And some excellent Receipts in Cookery, Physick, and Surgery. With many other useful Things never before printed.

London : printed for J. Stone, at Bedford-Row, near Gray's-Inn ; and sold by G. Strahan, at the Royal-Exchange ; W. Mears, on Ludgate-Hill ; J. Jackson, in Pall-Mall ; C. Corbet, at Temple-Bar ; and T. Boreman, near Child's Coffee-House, in St. Paul's Church-Yard. 1735.
(Price 2s. 6d.)

The cookery recipes are comparatively few. The medical ones include the juice of wood-lice and the use of animal dung with new and disgusting variants. The most extraordinary chapter is one not mentioned on the title-page. It is called the Vermin-killer and contains wonderful recipes said to be approved by Pliny, Cornelius Agrippa, Paxamus, Dydimus, and other learned writers.

1736 THE COMPLETE FAMILY-PIECE :
and, Country Gentleman, and Farmer's Best Guide.
In Three Parts.
Part I. Containing a very choice and valuable Collection of near Eight Hundred well-experienced Practical Family-Receipts in Physick and Surgery ; Cookery, Pastry and Confectionary, with a complete Bill of Fare for every Month in the Year, and Instructions for placing the Dishes on a Table ; for Pickling and Preserving all Sorts of Fruits, Tongues, Hams, &c., for Distilling and Fermenting of all Compound, Simple Waters and Spirits ; for making Mum, Cyder and Perry, Mead and Metheglin ; and for making and preserving all Sorts of excellent English Wines ; with good and useful Instructions for Brewing fine, strong, good, wholesome and palatable Drinks, as Beers, Ales, &c., in

small Quantities, and at easy Rates, for the Use of all private Families; with divers other useful and valuable Receipts interspersed through the Whole, particularly Dr. Mead's for the Cure of the Bite of a Mad Dog: Many of which were never before Printed, and the others experimentally taken from the latest and very best Authorities; and being all regularly digested under their proper Heads, are divided into six different Chapters.

Part II. Containing,

  I. Full Instructions to be observed in Hunting, Coursing, Setting and Shooting; with an Account of the several Kinds of Dogs necessary for those Diversions, and Receipts for the Cure of all common Distempers to which they are liable; as also Receipts for the Cleaning and Preserving of Boots, Fire-Arms, &c.

 II. Cautions, Rules and Directions to be taken and observed in Fishing; with the Manner of making and preserving of Rods, Lines, Floats, Artificial Flies, &c., and for chusing and preserving several Sorts of curious Baits.

III. A full and complete Kalendar of all Work necessary to be done in the Fruit, Flower, and Kitchen Gardens, Green-House, &c., with the Produce of each, in every Month throughout the whole Year.

Part III. Containing practical Rules, and Methods, for the Improving of Land, and Managing a Farm in all its Branches; with several curious Receipts for Brining, Liming and preparing Wheat, Barley, Oats, &c., for Sowing; excellent Receipts for destroying of Rats and Mice; a great Number of choice Receipts for the Cure of all common Distempers incident to all Sorts of Cattle; and a complete Kalender of all Business necessary to be done in the Field, Yard, &c., by the Farmer, in every Month throughout the Year.

With a complete Alphabetical Index to each Part.

The Whole, being faithfully Collected by several very

eminent and ingenious Gentlemen, is now first published, at their earnest Desire, for the general Benefit of Mankind. London, printed and sold by T. Longman, at the Ship in Pater-noster Row. 1736. (Price bound 3s. 6d.)

The second edition was 1737.

As the title-page indicates, this is a very comprehensive work. The medical portion, according to the preface, is recommended to 'many pious and charitable Gentlewomen in the Country that are blessed with Riches, and make it almost their constant Business and Study to prepare and give Physick to the Poor, for almost all Distempers'. The dung of various animals and other horrible things are ingredients in many of the recipes. The cookery portion is comparatively small.

1736 THE ACCOMPLISH'D HOUSEWIFE, AND HOUSE-KEEPER'S POCKET-COMPANION,

or, The Compleat Family Cook.

Containing several Hundred Curious, and the most, Useful Receipts in

Cookery,	Pastry,
Pickling,	Jellies,
Preserving,	Syrups,
Candying,	English Wines, &c.

With Plain and Easy Directions for Dressing and Preparing every Thing suitable and necessary for an Elegant Entertainment, from Two to Five or Ten Dishes, &c., and Instructions for Placing them in their proper order on the Table.

Also, Bills of Fare for every Month in the Year, in such a copious and useful Manner, that no Person need be at a Loss for an agreeable Variety of Dishes.

To which are added many Excellent Prescriptions of approved Receipts, from the most Eminent Physicians, for most Distempers incident to the Human Body.

Printed by the Author, in the Year 1736.

(Price 1s. 6d. bound.)

A duodecimo of 155 pages. Snails boiled with daisies are recommended for consumption.

1736 DICTIONARIUM DOMESTICUM,
being a New and Compleat Household Dictionary, for the Use both of City and Country, shewing,

I. The whole Arts of Brewing, Baking, Cookery, and Pickling. Also Confectionary in its several Branches.
II. The Management of the Kitchen, Pantry, Larder, Dairy, Olitory, and Poultry. With the proper Seasons for Flesh, Fowl and Fish.
III. The Herdsman : Giving an Account of the Diseases of Cattle, Poultry, &c. And the most approved Remedies for their Cure.
IV. The English Vineyard ; being the best Method of making English Wines and of Distilling most Kinds of Simple and Compound Cordial Waters.
V. The Apiary : Or, The Manner of Breeding, Hiving and managing of Bees.
VI. The Family Physician and Herbalist : Containing the choicest Collection of Receipts for most Distempers, incident to Human Bodies, hitherto made Publick ; with the Qualities and Uses of Physical Herbs and Plants of English Growth.

By N. Bailey, Author of the Universal Etymological English Dictionary.
London, printed for C. Hitch at the Red-Lion, and C. Davis, both in Patei-Noster-Row ; and S. Austen at the Angel and Bible, in St. Paul's Church-Yard. MDCCXXXVI.

There is a frontispiece of a lady in her kitchen, dairy, &c. Nathan Bailey was a schoolmaster at Stepney. He died in 1742.

1737 THE WHOLE DUTY OF A WOMAN :
or, an infallible Guide to the Fair Sex, Containing, Rules, Directions, and Observations, for their Conduct and Behaviour through all Ages and Circumstances of Life, as Virgins, Wives, or Widows. With Directions, how to obtain all Useful and Fashionable Accomplishments suitable

to the Sex. In which are comprised all Parts of Good Housewifery, particularly Rules and Receipts in every Kind of Cookery.

1. Making all Sorts of Soops and Sauces.
2. Dressing Flesh, Fish, and Fowl; this last illustrated with Cuts, shewing how every Fowl, Wild or Tame, is to be trust for the Spit: Likewise all other Kind of Game.
3. Making above 40 different sorts of Puddings.
4. The Whole Art of Pastry in making Pies, Tarts, and Pasties.
5. Receipts for all Manner of Pickling, Collaring, &c.
6. For Preserving, making Creams, Jellies, and all Manner of Confectionary.
7. Rules and Directions for setting out Dinners, Suppers, and Grand Entertainments.

To which is added, Bills of Fare for every Month in the Year, curiously engraven on Copper Plates, with the Forms of Tables and Dishes, and the Shapes of Pies, Tarts, and Pasties. With Instructions for Marketing.

Also Rules and Receipts for making all the choicest Cordials for the Closet : Brewing Beers, Ales, &c. Making all Sorts of English Wines, Cyder, Mum, Mead, Metheglin, Vinegar, Verjuice, Catchup, &c. With some fine Perfumes, Pomatums, Cosmeticks and other Beautifiers.

London, printed for T. Read, in Dogwell-Court, White-Fryers, Fleet-Street. MDCCXXXVII.

A second edition was published in 1740 under a new title, THE LADY'S COMPANION. This book is a much larger book than 'The whole Duty of a Woman' of 1701. It resembles it in having preliminary chapters on moral conduct, but cookery takes up the greater part of the work.

1740 AN ALARM TO ALL PERSONS

touching their Health and Lives : or, A Discovery of the most shocking, pernicious, and destructive Practices made use of by many in this Kingdom, who make and sell divers Kinds

of Eatables and Drinkables; whereby many languish in their Health, and lose their Lives; founded on Verity and Facts. By Jasper Arnaud, sometime past First Cook to the late Duke of Orleans, and now for some Time Cook in London. To which are added, Remarks on the Nature of the destructive Ingredients made use of in the abovesaid Practices in Relation to Health: Communicated to the Author by a Learned Physician.
London, printed for T. Payne, in Round-Court in the Strand, opposite York-Buildings. M DCC XL.

A pamphlet of 24 pages on adulteration.

1740 (?) E. KIDDER'S RECEIPTS OF PASTRY AND COOKERY,
for the Use of his Scholars. Who teaches at his School in St. Martins le Grand: on Mondays, Tuesdays, & Wednesdays, in the Afternoon. Also on Thursdays, Fridays & Saturdays, in the Afternoon, at his School next to Furnivals Inn in Holborn. Ladies may be taught at their own Houses.

There is a frontispiece of the author by Rob. Sheppard. Another edition is slightly enlarged. The whole book is engraved and printed on one side of the page.

1741 THE FAMILY MAGAZINE:
in Two Parts.

Part I.

Containing Useful Directions in All the Branches of House-Keeping and Cookery. Particularly Shewing how to Buy-in the Best of all Sorts of Provisions; As Poultry-Ware, Butchers-Meat, Fish, Fruit, &c.
With several Hundred Receipts in

Cookery,	Distilling,
Pastry,	Brewing,
Pickling,	Cosmeticks, &c.
Confectionary,	

Together with the Art of making English Wines, &c.

Part II.

Containing A Compendious Body of Physick; Succinctly Treating of all the Diseases and Accidents incident to Men, Women, and Children: with Practical Rules and Directions for the Preserving and Restoring of Health, and Prolonging of Life.

In a Method intirely New and Intelligible; in which every Disease is rationally and practically considered, in its several Stages and Changes; and approved Recipe's inserted under every Distemper, in Alphabetical Order. Being principally the Common-place Book of a late able Physician, by which he successfully, for many Years, regulated his Practice.

With a Supplement, containing a great Variety of Experienced Receipts, from Two Excellent Family Collections.

Now First communicated for the Publick Benefit.

To which is Added, An Explanation of such Terms of Art used in the Work, as could not be so easily reduced to the Understanding of common Readers.

London, printed for J. Osborn, at the Golden-Ball in Paternoster-Row. M DCC XLI.

Other editions are 1743 (2), 1754 (4). The preface is signed 'Arabella Atkyns', which the B. M. catalogue says is a pseudonym. In it she states that the medical portion, which is much larger than the cookery, is taken from a common-place book of her brother who was a physician. It may be mentioned that she is the first lady who apologizes for her boldness in venturing to treat certain maladies which a lady would hardly be expected to include. The cookery part is well arranged, the medical part is full of horrors. The treatment for appendicitis is to 'apply a live puppy to the naked belly' and follow up with a cataplasm of rotten apples or of 'sheeps-dung boil'd with milk'.

ENGLISH COOKERY BOOKS

1743 A PRESENT FOR A SERVANT-MAID,
or, The Sure Means of gaining Love and Esteem.
Under the following Heads:

Observance.
Avoiding Sloth.
Sluttishness.
Staying on Errands.
Telling Family Affairs.
Secrets among Fellow-Servants.
Entering into their Quarrels.
Tale-bearing.
Being an Eye-Servant.
Carelessness of Children.
Of Fire, Candle, Thieves.
New Acquaintance.
Fortune-Tellers.
Giving Saucy Answers.
Liquorishness.
Apeing the Fashion.
Dishonesty.
The Market-Penny.
Delaying to give Change.
Giving away Victuals.
Bringing in Chair-women.
Washing Victuals.
Quarrels with Fellow-Servants.
Behaviour to the Sick.
Hearing Things against a Master or Mistress.
Being too free with Men-Servants.
Conduct towards Apprentices.
Mispending Time.
Publick Shews.
Vails.
Giving Advice too freely.
Chastity.
Temptations from the Master.
If a Single Man.
If a Married Man.
If from the Master's Son.
If from Gentlemen Lodgers.

To which are added Directions for going to Market: Also, For Dressing any Common Dish, whether Flesh, Fish or Fowl.

With some Rules for Washing, &c.

The whole calculated for making both the Mistress and the Maid happy.

London, printed and publish'd by T. Gardner, at Cowley's Head, without Temple-Bar; and sold by the Booksellers of Town and Country, 1743.

(Price One Shilling, or 25 for a Guinea to those who give them away.)

An edition was published in Dublin in 1744. It is a very entertaining little book, but the cookery portion is not of much account.

1743 THE INSTRUCTOR,
or, Young Man's Best Companion.
By George Fisher.
The Seventh Edition.

The full title-page is not given as the amount of cookery is very small. The B. M. catalogue states that the book is by Mrs. Slack. It ran through more than thirty editions, and was reprinted in 1853.

1744 THE ART OF PRESERVING HEALTH.
By John Armstrong, M.D.
London, printed for A. Millar. 1744.

A poem. The second book relates to diet. There are several editions.

1744 ADAM'S LUXURY, AND EVE'S COOKERY;
or, The Kitchen-Garden display'd.
In Two Parts.
   I. Shewing the best and most approved Methods of raising and bringing to the greatest Perfection, all the Products of the Kitchen-Garden; with a Kalendar shewing the different Products of each Month, and the Business proper to be done in it.
   II. Containing a large Collection of Receipts for dressing all Sorts of Kitchen-Stuff, so as to afford a great Variety of cheap, healthful, and palatable Dishes.

To which is added, The Physical Virtues of every Herb and Root.

Designed for the Use of all who would live Cheap, and preserve their Health to old Age; particularly for Farmers and Tradesmen in the Country, who have but small Pieces of Garden Ground, and are willing to make the most of it. London, printed for R. Dodsley, in Pall-Mall; and Sold by M. Cooper, at the Globe in Pater-noster Row. M DCC XLIV.

There is a half-title, 'Adam's Luxury, and Eve's Cookery'. It is not a vegetarian hand-book, as meat gravies are used in the recipes.

1745 THE ACCOMPLISH'D HOUSEWIFE ;
or, The Gentleman's Companion : Containing

I. Reflections on the Education of the Fair Sex ; with Characters for their Imitation.
II. The Penman's Advice to the Ladies ; or the Art of Writing made easy, and entertaining.
III. Instructions for addressing Persons of Distinction, in Writing or Discourse.
IV. An easy Introduction to the Study of Practical Arithmetic.
V. Directions for Copying Prints or Drawings, and Painting either in Oil or Water Colours, or with Crayons.
VI. Directions for Marketing, with respect to Butcher's Meat, Poulterer's Ware, and Fish.
VII. A Bill of Fare for every Month in the Year.
VIII. Receipts in Cookery, Pastry, &c.
IX. Instructions for Carving and placing Dishes on the Table.
X. All Sorts of Pickles, Made Wines, &c.
XI. Remarks on the Nature and Qualities of the most common aliments.
XII. Recipes in Physick and Surgery.
XIII. Remarks on the Causes and Symptoms of most Diseases.
XIV. The Florist's Kalendar.
XV. Familiar Letters on several Occasions in common Life ; with Instructions to young Orphan Ladies how to judge of Proposals of Marriage made to them without the Consent of their Friends or Guardians.
XVI. A Dictionary serving for the Translation of ordinary English Words into more scholastic ones.

Concluding with some serious Instructions for the Conduct of the Fair Sex, with regard to their Duty towards God, and towards their Neighbours.

London, printed for J. Newberry, at the Bible and Sun near the Chapter-House in St. Paul's Church-yard. M DCC XLV.

The cookery part is simple and a note at the end of the recipes in physic recommends those who want ' a larger System of Cookery, Physick, &c. ' to consult the House-keeper's Pocket-Book by Mrs. Harrison.

1745 THE PYTHAGOREAN DIET OF VEGETABLES ONLY,

conducive to the Preservation of Health, and the Cure of Diseases.

A Discourse delivered at Florence, in the Month of August, 1743.

By Antonio Cocchi, of Mugello.

Translated from the Italian.

R. Dodsley. 1745.

> A vegetarian pamphlet. There are no recipes in it.

1747 THE ART OF COOKERY MADE PLAIN AND EASY;

Which far exceeds any Thing of the Kind ever yet Published. Containing,

I. Of Roasting, Boiling, &c.
II. Of Made-Dishes.
III. Read this Chapter, and you will find how Expensive a French Cook's Sauce is.
IV. To make a number of pretty little Dishes fit for a Supper, or Side-Dish, and little Corner-Dishes for a great Table; and the rest you have in the Chapter for Lent.
V. To dress Fish.
VI. Of Soops and Broths.
VII. Of Puddings.
VIII. Of Pies.
IX. For a Fast-Dinner, a Number of good Dishes, which you may make use for a Table at any other Time.
X. Directions for the Sick.
XI. For Captains of Ships.
XII. Of Hog's Puddings, Sausages, &c.
XIII. To Pot and Make Hams, &c.
XIV. Of Pickling.
XV. Of Making Cakes, &c.
XVI. Of Cheesecakes, Creams, Jellies, Whip Syllabubs, &c.
XVII. Of Made Wines, Brewing, French Bread, Muffins, &c.
XVIII. Jarring Cherries, and Preserves, &c.
XIX. To Make Anchovies, Vermicella, Ketchup, Vinegar, and to keep Artichokes, French-Beans, &c.
XX. Of Distilling.
XXI. How to Market, and the Seasons of the Year

for Butcher's Meat, Poultry, Fish, Herbs, Roots, and Fruit.

XXII. A certain Cure for the Bite of a Mad Dog. By Dr. Mead.

By a Lady.

London, printed for the Author ; and sold at Mrs. Ashburn's, a China Shop Corner of Fleet-Ditch. M DCC XLVII.

(Price 3s. stitch'd, and 5s. bound.)

And at Mrs. Wharton's, at the Blue-coat Boy, near the Royal Exchange.

This is the first edition of the famous book by Mrs. Hannah Glasse. It is a small folio, but the other editions are octavo ; 1747 (2), 1748 (3), 1751 (4), 1755 (5), 1758 (6), 1760 (7), 1763 (8), 1765 (9). Besides these there are many other editions generally called ' new ', 1767, 1770, 1774, 1778, 1784, 1788, 1796, 1803.

1749 THE LONDON AND COUNTRY COOK :
or, Accomplished Housewife, containing practical Directions and the best Receipts in all the Branches of Cookery and Housekeeping ; such as

Boiling,
Roasting,
Pastry,
Pickling,
Jellies,
Preserving,

Confectionary,
Cakes,
Creams,
Cordials,
Syrups,
English Wines, &c.

Intersperced with many sovereign and approved Medicines used by Private Families in most Distempers ; and illustrated with Forty-nine large Copper Plates. By Charles Carter, cook to his Grace the Duke of Argyle, &c. The Third Edition.

Revised and much improved by a Gentlewoman ; many Years Housekeeper to an eminent Merchant in the City of London. London, printed for Charles Hitch in Pater-noster Row ; Stephen Austen in Newgate-street, and John Hinton in St. Paul's Church-yard. M DCC XLIX.

This is a different book from ' The Compleat City and Country Cook ', although the plates are the same.

1749 ENGLISH HOUSEWIFERY,

exemplified in above Four Hundred and Fifty Receipts, giving Directions in most Parts of Cookery; and how to prepare various Sorts of

Soops,	Cakes,
Made-Dishes,	Creams,
Pastes,	Jellies,
Pickles,	Made-Wines, &c.

With Cuts for the orderly placing the Dishes and Courses; also Bills of Fare for every Month in the Year; and an alphabetical Index to the Whole.

A Book necessary for Mistresses of Families, higher and lower Women Servants, and confined to Things Useful, Substantial and Splendid, and calculated for the Preservation of Health, and upon the Measures of Frugality, being the Result of thirty Years Practice and Experience.

By Elizabeth Moxon.

Leedes, printed by James Lister, 1749.

The second, third, fourth, and fifth editions are undated. In the second and third the name is spelled Elisabeth. On the title-pages of these editions it is stated that the book is 'sold by the author at Pontefract', which was, therefore, probably her residence.

In 1758 appeared a supplement:

English Housewifery Improved; or, a Supplement to Moxon's Cookery, containing upwards of Sixty Modern and Valuable Receipts in

Pastry,	Made Dishes,
Preserving,	Made Wines, &c.

Collected by a Person of Judgment.

Leedes, printed by Griffith Wright, for George Copperthwaite, Bookseller, M DCC LVIII.

This supplement is found both by itself and also bound with the eighth edition (1758) of the main work.

Other editions of the book and its supplement are 1764 (9 and 2), 1769 (10 and 3), 1785 (12 and 3), 1789 (13 and 5).

There is also an edition of 1778 (12 and 5) which bears no publisher's name and seems to be spurious. Another suspicious edition is the fourteenth with no date, 'by Elizabeth Moxon, and Others. Printed and sold by Andrew Hambleton'.

1750 THE COUNTRY HOUSEWIFE'S FAMILY COMPANION;

or, Profitable Directions for whatever relates to the Management and Good Œconomy of the Domestick Concerns of a Country Life, according to the Present Practice of the Country Gentleman's, the Yeoman's, the Farmer's, &c. Wives, in the Counties of Hertford, Bucks, and other Parts of England: shewing how great Savings may be made in Housekeeping: and wherein, among many others, the following Heads are particularly treated of and explained:

I. The Preservation and Improvement of Wheat, Barley, Rye, Oats, and other Meals; with Directions for making several Sorts of Bread, Cakes, Puddings, Pies, &c.

II. Frugal Management of Meats, Fruits, Roots, and all Sorts of Herbs; best Methods of Cookery; and a Cheap Way to make Soups, Sauces, Gruels, &c.

III. Directions for the Farm Yard; with the best Method of increasing and fatning all Sorts of Poultry, as Turkies, Geese, Ducks, Fowls, &c.

IV. The best Way to breed and fatten Hogs; sundry curious and Cheap Methods of preparing Hog's Meat; Directions for curing Bacon, Brawn, pickled Pork, Hams, &c., with the Management of Sows and Pigs.

V. The best Method of making Butter and Cheese, with several curious Particulars containing the whole management of the Dairy.

VI. The several Ways of making good Malt; with Directions for brewing good Beer, Ale, &c.

With Variety of Curious Matters, wherein are contained frugal Methods for victualling Harvest-men, Ways to destroy all Sorts of Vermine, the best Manner of suckling and fattening Calves, Prescriptions for curing all Sorts of Distempers in Cattle, with Variety of curious Receits for Pickling, Preserving, Distilling, &c.

The Whole founded on near thirty Years Experience by W. Ellis, Farmer, at Little Gaddesden, near Hempsted, Hertfords.

London, printed for James Hodges, at the Looking-glass, facing St. Magnus Church, London-Bridge; and B. Collins, Bookseller, at Salisbury. 1750.

There is a farm-yard scene as frontispiece. The book is made interesting by many extraordinary anecdotes. One is of a man named James Silcock of Hinton in Wiltshire, who, ' being very much accustomed to eat Horse-flesh and Dog-flesh, did undertake to eat a Frog and a Mole; after he had eat the Mole, the Person that undertook to provide the Frog, by mistake brought a Toad, which he having eaten, and swallowed a Plenty of Liquor, immediately died'. The medical recipes, many of the usual filthy nature, are plentifully illustrated by reports of cures.

1750 A COLLECTION OF SCARCE AND VALUABLE RECEIPTS,

never before printed, and taken from the Manuscripts of divers Persons of the most refin'd Taste and greatest Judgment in the Arts of Cookery, Preserving, &c.

To which is added, the Author's own Method of Pickling, together with Directions for making several Sorts of Wines, Mead, Sherbet, Punch, &c. after the most approved Manner.

Concluding with many excellent Prescriptions, of singular Efficacy in most Distempers, incident to the Human Body. By Anne Battam, Mistress of Myon's Coffee-House, in Great-Russel-street, Bloomsbury; where the said Book may be had.

London, printed for the Author. M DCC L.

(Price Three Shillings.)

A second edition, much enlarged, was published in 1759. The title-page speaks of the 'late' Mrs. Anne Battam.

1750 (c.) THE MODERN METHOD OF REGULATING AND FORMING A TABLE,

explained and displayed, containing a great Variety of Dinners laid out in the most elegant Taste, from two Courses of Five and Five, to Twenty-one and Twenty-one

Dishes; finely represented, on One Hundred and Fifty-Two Copper Plates. Together with Twelve elegant Dinners for different Seasons of the Year and a correct List of such Particulars as are in Season during every Month. The whole calculated for the Use and Ease of Ladies, Clerks of the Kitchen, House-keepers, &c.

By several eminent Cooks, and others well acquainted with these Arts.

Printed for J. Hughes, opposite the Duke of Grafton's, in Old Bond-Street; and S. Crowder, No. 12, Pater-noster-Row.

This is a large folio entirely devoted to the various ways of laying out a dining-table.

1750 (c.) THE ART OF CONFECTIONARY:
shewing the Various Methods of Preserving all Sorts of Fruits, Dry and Liquid;

Oranges,	Almonds,	Peaches,
Lemons,	Goosberries,	Walnuts,
Citrons,	Cherries,	Nectarines,
Golden-Pippins,	Currants,	Figs,
Wardens,	Plumbs,	Grapes, &c.
Apricots Green,	Rasberries,	

Also Flowers and Herbs, as Violets, Angelica, Orange Flowers, &c. With Directions for making all Sorts of Biscakes, Maspins, Sugar-Works, and Candies;

The best Methods of Clarifying, and the different Ways of boiling Sugar;

And many curious and well-experienced Receipts for making Cordial Waters, and British Wines, from Fruits, Flowers, and Herbs.

By the late ingenious Mr. Edward Lambert, Confectioner, in Pall-Mall.

To which is now added The Ladies Toilet or The Art of Preserving Beauty.

London, printed for F. Newbery, at the Corner of St. Paul's Church-Yard.

[Price One Shilling.]

A book of 63 pages. The beauty recipes seem fairly good.

1750 (c.) THE PRUDENT HOUSEWIFE:
or, Complete English Cook for Town and Country. Being the newest Collection of the most Genteel, and least expensive Receipts in every Branch of Cookery, viz.

Going to Market;

| For Roasting, Boiling, | Frying, Hashing, Stewing, | Broiling, Baking, Fricasseeing. |

Also for

| Making Puddings, Custards, Cakes, | Cheese-Cakes, Pies, Tarts, Ragouts, | Soups, Jellies, Syllabubs, Wines, &c. |

To which are added, selected from the Papers of a Lady of Distinction, lately deceased, New and Infallible Rules to be observed in

| Pickling, | Preserving, | Brewing, &c. |

And, in order to render it still more valuable than any other Publication that hath appeared, a Treasure of Valuable Medicines, for the Cure of every Disorder, crowns the whole of this Work; which contains every Instruction that relates to the pleasing of the Palate, and the Preservation of that inestimable Blessing, Health.

Written by Mrs. Fisher, of Richmond.

London, printed by T. Sabine, No. 17, Little New-street, Shoe Lane, Fleet-street: Where Printing is expeditiously performed in all its Branches, on reasonable Terms.

Price One Shilling.

There is a frontispiece representing a kitchen. This is a little book of 136 pages, the medical portion being excellent and far above any preceding book. The symptoms of the diseases are given and then the remedies to be applied. The greater number of the remedies are really good.

1753 THE YOUNG WOMAN'S COMPANION ;
or the Servant-Maid's Assistant ; digested under the several Heads hereinafter mentioned,
Viz.

I. A Short Essay on the Benefits of Learning, &c. by way of Introduction.
II. The Young Woman's Guide to the Knowledge of her Mother-Tongue.
III. A compendious English Spelling Dictionary, peculiarly calculated for the present Undertaking.
IV. An easy Introduction to the Art of Writing, with Rules of Life.
V. Familiar Letters on various Subjects.
VI. The Young Woman's Guide to the Art of Numbers, with a great Variety of useful Tables.
VII. The Compleat Market Woman, with proper Instructions to prevent the Purchaser from being imposed upon.
VIII. The Compleat Cook-Maid, Pastry-Cook, and Confectioner.
IX. Advice to Servants in General, with Respect to their Duty towards God, their Employers, and themselves, with additional Prayers and Hymns.

and lastly a compleat Table of the Contents.

The whole compiled by Mary Johnson, for many Years a Superintendent of a Lady of Quality's Family in the City of York.

London, printed for H. Jeffery, in Mercer's Chapel, Cheapside. M DCC LIII.

There is a portrait of the authoress as frontispiece with the lettering ' Madam Johnson the accomplish'd Lady '.

A second edition appeared in 1759 under the title of MADAM JOHNSON'S PRESENT. It has many points of difference from the original. Other editions are 1765 (3), 1766 (4), 1772 (6). Probably all the editions contained the portrait.

This is an entertaining book and must have been useful in its day. Its moral standpoint throughout is that of ' The Compleat

Servant-maid' of 1677, and may be summed up in one of its own adages, 'Be content in that Station which Providence has allotted you'.

1753 THE LADY'S COMPANION,

containing upwards of Three Thousand different Receipts in every kind of Cookery and those the most fashionable; being Four Times the Quantity of any Book of this Sort.

I. Making near two Hundred different Sorts of Soops, Pottages, Broths, Sauces, Cullises, &c., after the French, Italian, Dutch, and English Way; also making Cake Soop for the Pocket.

II. Dressing Flesh, Fish, and Fowl; this last illustrated with Cuts, shewing how every Fowl is to be truss'd.

III. Directions for making Ragoos and Fricaseys.

IV. Directions for Dressing all manner of Kitchen Garden Stuff, &c.

V. Making two Hundred different Sorts of Puddings, Florendines, Tanzeys, &c., which are four Times the number to be met with in any other Book of this Kind.

VI. The whole Art of Pastry, in making upwards of two Hundred Pies, (with the Shapes of them engraven on Copper-Plates) Tarts, Pasties, Custards, Cheese-Cakes, Yorkshire Muffins, &c.

VII. Receipts for all Manner of Pickling, Potting, Collaring, &c.

VIII. For Preserving, making Creams, Jellies, and all Manner of Confectionary, with particular Receipts for making Orgeat and Blanc Manger.

IX. Rules and Directions for setting out Dinners, Suppers, and grand Entertainments.

To which is added Bills of Fare for every Month in the Year. Also Directions for Brewing Beers, Ales, &c. making all Sorts of English Wines, Cyder, Mum, Metheglin, Vinegar, Verjuice, Catchup, &c. With the Receipts of Mrs. Stephens for the Stone; Dr. Mead for the Bite of a Mad Dog; the Recipe, sent from Ireland, for the Gout; Sir Hans Sloane's Receipt for Sore Eyes; and the Receipt for making Tar Water.

The Sixth Edition, with large Additions.
Vol. I.
London, printed for J. Hodges, on London-Bridge ; and R. Baldwin, at the Rose, in Pater-noster Row. 1753.

This seems a very comprehensive cookery book, but unfortunately the second volume has never turned up.

1753 THE FAMILY'S BEST FRIEND :
or the whole Art of Cookery made Plain and Easy ; in a method intirely new and suited to every Capacity.
By his Majestys Authority.
Calculated for the Preservation of Health, and upon the principles of Frugality.
Containing compleat directions in the various Branches of Cookery, Pickleing and Preserving ; also in the making of Cakes, Creams, Jellies, Soops, Pastes, and all Sorts of Made Wines, &c. The whole exemplified in above Five Hundred choice Receipts : being the Result of above thirty Years Practice and Experience ; together with an attentive Observation of all the Books hitherto published in Cookery.
To which is added, a Remedy for preventing Persons from catching the Small-Pox, Plague, or any Epidemical Disorder ; Dr. Mead's Cure for the Bite of a Mad Dog ; and Instructions for preparing such Diets as are proper for Sick Persons.
As also, a valuable Receipt for taking Iron Moulds out of all kinds of Linnen, without the least Prejudice to the Cloth tho' ever so fine, &c. &c. &c.
By Arabella Fairfax.
The Fifth Edition, Price Two Shillings sew'd.
London, printed for the Author only. 1753.

The preface is printed in a peculiar type 'in order to prevent unfair Traders from reprinting, or in any wise defrauding the Author or the Publick, by publishing the Whole or any Part of this Book, in an injudicious incorrect Manner '.

1754 THE DIRECTOR:

or, Young Woman's Best Companion, containing above Three Hundred easy Receipts in Cookery, Pastry, Preserving, Candying, Pickling, Collaring, Physick, and Surgery.

To which are added, plain and easy Instructions for chusing Beef, Mutton, Veal, Fish, Fowl, and all other Eatables:

Also, Directions for Carving, and Made Wines: likewise Bills of Fare for every Month in the Year. With a complete Index to the Whole.

A Book necessary for all Families.

By Sarah Jackson.

Collected for the Use of her own Family, and printed at the Request of her Friends.

Being one of the Plainest and Cheapest of the Kind.

The Whole makes a complete Family Cook and Physician.

London, printed for J. Fuller, at his Circulating Library in Butcher-hall-lane, near Newgate-street; and S. Neale, Bookseller, at Chatham. MDCCLIV.

> From a notice at the beginning it seems that the work came out in weekly parts. It is a little book of 112 pages. Wood-lice, snails, and pigeon's dung are part of the pharmacopoeia.

1755 COOKERY REFORMED:

or The Lady's Assistant. Containing a select Number of the best and most approved Receipts in Cookery, Pastry, Preserving, Candying, Pickling, &c.

Together with a distinct Account of the Nature of Aliments, and what are most suitable to every Constitution.

Published from Papers collected by several Gentlemen and Ladies eminent for their good Sense and Œconomy.

To which is added the Family Physician; comprehending an easy, safe and certain Method of curing most Diseases incident to the Human Body.

Published at the Request of a Physician of great Experience, who for the Benefit of the Purchaser, has carefully corrected this Work ; and shewn why several things heretofore used in Cookery, and inserted in other Books, have been prejudicial to Mankind.

London, printed for P. Davey and B. Law, at the Bible and Ball in Avemary Lane, M DCC LV.

<small>The cookery occupies 254 pages, and the Family Physician, separately paged, 114.</small>

1756 THE LADIES COMPANION ;
or, The Housekeeper's Guide : being a Magazine of such Choice Matters, as the Housekeeper ought not to be without ; and what will compleatly accomplish the Young Servant for the best of Families. Containing, among a Variety of other Things, all that concerns,

Cookery,	Pickling,
Confectionary,	Cordials,
Preserving,	Made Wines,
Pastry,	Brewing, &c.

With a great Variety of other Materials as will be found both Necessary and Valuable.

Particularly, an excellent Method for Preserving of Metals from Rust, such as Guns, Grates, Candlesticks, &c. found out by Mons. Millien, for which he receiv'd a Reward of 10,000*l*. by the Royal Academy of Paris.

In this Book is shewn, the most certain and best Method for the Management of a good Beer Cellar : How to restore sour Beer to its first Perfection ; and how to keep Beer or Ale always very fine.

Also an extraordinary good way of Preserving a constant Stock of Yeast.

By a Gentlewoman,

Who has been a Housekeeper to several Noble Families many Years.

London.

<small>Unfortunately the copy of the book, from which the title has been taken, has been cut down so that neither printer nor date appear. The date has been noted from another copy.</small>

1758 THE ART OF COOKERY,

containing above Six Hundred and Fifty of the most approv'd Receipts heretofore published, under the following Heads, viz.

Roasting,	Cakes,	Pickling,
Boiling,	Cheese-Cakes,	Preserving,
Frying,	Tarts,	Pastry,
Broiling,	Pyes,	Collering,
Baking,	Soops,	Confectionary,
Fricasees,	Made-Wines,	Creams,
Puddings,	Jellies,	Ragoos,
Custards,	Candying,	Brasing, &c. &c.

Also, a Bill of Fare for every Month in the Year, with an Alphabetical Index to the Whole:

Being a Book highly necessary for all Families, having the Grounds of Cookery fully display'd therein.

By John Thacker, Cook to the Honourable and Reverend the Dean and Chapter in Durham.

Newcastle upon Tyne: Printed by I. Thompson and Company. M DCC LVIII.

> The author apologizes in his preface for adding another to the many cookery books already existing on the ground that the latter 'are far short of being generally useful, especially in these Northern Parts, where the Seasons occasion such Alterations in the Bills of Fare for each Month, from those calculated for the Southern Parts'.

1759 A NEW AND EASY METHOD OF COOKERY,

treating,

I. Of Gravies, Soups, Broths, &c.
II. Of Fish, and their Sauces.
III. To Pot and Make Hams, &c.
IV. Of Pies, Pasties, &c.
V. Of Pickling and Preserving.
VI. Of Made Wines, Distiling and Brewing, &c.

To which are added, by Way of Appendix, Fifty-Three New and Useful Receipts, and Directions for Carving.

By Elizabeth Cleland.

ENGLISH COOKERY BOOKS 89

Chiefly intended for the Benefit of the Young Ladies who attend Her School.

The Second Edition.

Edinburgh, printed by C. Wright and Company : and sold at their Printing-house in Craig's Close, and by the Booksellers in Town. M DCC LIX.

> There are recipes for making a ' Crokain ', ' Fairy Butter ', and ' Whetstone Cakes '. A ' Mutchkin ' is often used as a measure.

1759 A COMPLETE SYSTEM OF COOKERY,

in which is set forth, a Variety of genuine Receipts, collected from several Years Experience under the celebrated Mr. de St. Clouet, sometime since Cook to his Grace the Duke of Newcastle.

By William Verral, Master of the White-Hart Inn in Lewes, Sussex.

Together with an Introductory Preface, shewing how every Dish is brought to Table, and in what Manner the meanest Capacity shall never err in doing what his Bill of Fare contains.

To which is added, a true Character of Mons. de St. Clouet. London, printed for the Author, and sold by him ; as also by Edward Verral Bookseller, in Lewes : and by John Rivington in St. Paul's Church-yard, London. M DCC LIX.

> The preface is very amusing, but does not give much information about St. Clouet, who was cook to the ' Marshal Richlieu '.

1760 THE SERVANT'S DIRECTORY,

or, House-Keeper's Companion : wherein the Duties of the

Chamber-Maid,	Landery-Maid,
Nursery-Maid,	Scullion, or
House-Maid,	Under-Cook,

Are fully and distinctly explained.

To which is annexed a Diary, or House-keeper's Pocket-Book for the whole Year.

With Directions for keeping Accounts with Tradesmen, and many other Particulars, fit to be known by the Mistress of a Family.

By H. Glass, Author of The Art of Cookery made plain and easy.

London, printed for the Author ; and sold by W. Johnston in Ludgate-street ; at Mrs. Wharton's, the Blue-Coat-Boys near the Royal-Exchange, at Mrs. Ashburnham's China-Shop the Corner of Fleet-Ditch, Mr. Vaughan's, Upholder in Prince's-street, Leicester-Fields, and by all the Booksellers in Town and Country.

N.B. This Book is entered in the Hall-book of the Company of Stationers.

The greater part of the book is taken up by the diary.

1760 (c.) THE COMPLETE CONFECTIONER :
or the Whole Art of Confectionary made Plain and Easy.

Shewing the various Methods of Preserving and Candying, both dry and liquid, all Kinds of Fruits, Flowers, and Herbs ; The different Ways of Clarifying Sugar ; and the Method of keeping Fruit, Nuts, and Flowers, fresh and fine all the Year round.

Also Directions for making

Rock-works and Candies,
Biscuits,
Rich Cakes,
Creams and Ice Creams,
Custards,
Jellies,
Blomonge,
Whip Syllabubs, and Cheese-cakes of all Sorts,
Sweetmeats,

English Wines of all Sorts,
Strong Cordials,
Simple Waters,
Mead, Oils, &c.
Syrups of all Kinds,
Milk Punch that will keep twenty Years,
Knicknacks and Trifles for Deserts, &c. &c. &c.

Likewise the Art of Making Artificial Fruit, with the Stalks in it, so as to resemble the natural Fruit.

ENGLISH COOKERY BOOKS

To which are added, some Bills of Fare for Deserts for Private Families.

By H. Glasse, Author of the Art of Cookery.

London, printed for J. Cooke, No. 17, Pater-noster Row.

Another edition appeared in 1772. In 1799 the book was issued in ten weekly parts, beginning with November 30, 'with considerable additions and corrections by Mrs. Maria Wilson,' and, bound in one volume, was published in 1800.

1760 (c.) THE TOWN AND COUNTRY COOK;
or, Young Woman's Best Guide, in the whole Art of Cookery, giving particular Directions for Roasting, Boiling, Broiling, Frying, and Stewing;

And the most approved Methods of making Hashes, Sauces, Gravies, Fricassees, Soups, &c. &c.

Together with the whole Art of Pastry; and the choicest Receipts for Cakes, &c.

To which are added many other Particulars.

London, printed for W. Lane, Leadenhall-Street, and sold by all other Booksellers.

(Price only Six-pence.)

A little book of 84 pages. There is a frontispiece representing a lady handing a paper or book to her cook.

1760 (c.) PROFESSED COOKERY:
containing

Boiling,	Pickling,
Roasting,	Potting,
Pastry,	Made-Wines,
Preserving,	Gellies,

And Part of Confectionaries.

With an Essay upon the Lady's Art of Cookery:

Together with a Plan of Housekeeping.

By Ann Cook, Teacher of the True Art of Cookery.

The Third Edition.

London, printed for and sold by the Author, at her Lodgings, in Mr. Moor's, Cabinet-maker, Fuller's Rents, Holborn. Price Six Shillings.

The book begins with a poem. Then follows a long essay criticizing some of the directions of Mrs. Glass. The Plan of Housekeeping, which ends the book, is in the form of a short story.

1762 THE LONDON COOK,
or the whole Art of Cookery made easy and familiar. Containing a great Number of approved and practical Receipts in every Branch of Cookery.

Viz.

Chap. I. Of Soups, Broths and Gravy.
II. Of Pancakes, Fritters, Possets, Tanseys, &c.
III. Of Fish.
IV. Of Boiling.
V. Of Roasting.
VI. Of Made-Dishes.
VII. Of Poultry and Game.
VIII. Sauces for Poultry and Game.
IX. Sauces for Butcher's Meat, &c.
X. Of Puddings.
XI. Of Pies, Custards, and Tarts, &c.
XII. Of Sausages, Hogs-Puddings, &c.
XIII. Of Potting and Collaring.
XIV. Of Pickles.
XV. Of Creams, Jellies, &c.
XVI. Of Made Wines.

By William Gelleroy, late Cook to her Grace the Dutchess of Argyle, and now to the Right Hon. Sir Samuel Fludger, Bart., Lord Mayor of the City of London.

To which is prefixed, a large Copper-Plate, representing his Majesty's Table, with its proper Removes, as it was served at Guild-Hall, on the 9th of November last, being the Lord Mayor's Day, when His Majesty, and the Royal Family, did the City the Honour to dine with them, and were highly pleased with their Entertainment.

London, printed for S. Crowder, and Co. at the Looking-glass; J. Coote, at the King's-Arms, in Pater-noster Row; and J. Fletcher, St. Paul's Church-Yard. M DCC LXII.

This seems a very good book and may be commended as being the first with a modest preface.

ENGLISH COOKERY BOOKS

1762 THE COMPLETE ENGLISH COOK ;
or Prudent Housewife. Being an entire New Collection of the most Genteel, yet least Expensive Receipts in every Branch of Cookery and good Housewifery.

viz.,

Roasting,	Fricaseys,	Potting,
Boiling,	Pies, Tarts,	Candying,
Stewing,	Puddings,	Collaring,
Ragoos,	Cheesecakes,	Pickling,
Soups,	Custards,	Preserving,
Sauces,	Jellies,	Made Wines, &c.

Together with the Art of Marketting, and Directions for placing Dishes on Table for Entertainments : Adorned with proper Cuts.
And many other Things equally Necessary.
The Whole made Easy to the Meanest Capacity, and far more Useful to Young Beginners than any Book of the kind ever yet published.

> In cooking Fowl, or Flesh, or Fish,
> Or any nice, or dainty Dish,
> With Care peruse this useful Book,
> 'Twill make you soon a perfect Cook.

By Catherine Brooks of Red-Lyon-Street.
To which is added, the Physical Director ; being near Two Hundred safe and certain Receipts for the Cure of most Disorders incident to the Human Body.
Also the whole Art of Clear-Starching, Ironing, &c.
The Second Edition, with the Addition of a great variety of Made Dishes, &c.
London, printed for the Authoress, and sold by J. Cooke, at Shakespear's-head, in Pater-noster-Row.
[Price One Shilling.]

The preface is dated Jan. 20, 1762. Each copy is signed by the Authoress. There is a frontispiece representing a kitchen with the lettering, ' She looketh well to the ways of her Household and eateth not the Bread of Idleness. Prov. 31. v. 27.' A fourth edition has the frontispiece reversed.

Two other editions, undated, are called ' The Experienced English Housekeeper ', and were probably issued after the appearance of Mrs. Raffald's book with that title in order to deceive. One was published at Manchester.

It is a duodecimo of 132 pages. The medical recipes are brief and authoritative, some being quite good. But it is difficult to believe that the use of a cold bath ' has cured a person of a Cancer in her Breast, a Consumption, a Sciatica, and Rheumatism, which she had near twenty years '.

1762 (c.) THE COMPLETE SERVANT MAID:
or Young Woman's best Companion.
Containing full, plain, and easy Directions for qualifying them for Service in General, but more especially for the Places of

> Lady's Woman, Laundry Maid,
> Housekeeper, Cook Maid,
> Chambermaid, Kitchen, or
> Nursery Maid, Scullery Maid,
> Housemaid, Dairy Maid.

To which are added, useful Instructions for discharging the Duties of each Character, with Reputation to themselves, and Satisfaction to their Employers.

Including a Variety of useful Receipts (proper to be known by all young Persons) particularly for cleaning Household Furniture, Silks, Laces, Gold, Silver, Wearing apparel, &c. &c.

By Mrs. Anne Barker, who having for many Years discharged the Office of Housekeeper in the most respectable Families, wishes to communicate her Experience to those of her own Sex, whose Circumstances oblige them to live in Servitude.

> Be honest and trusted—be prudent and prais'd,
> Be mild to be pleasing—and meek to be rais'd:
> For the Servant whose Diligence strikes Envy dumb,
> Shall in place be admir'd—and a Mistress become.

London, printed for J. Cooke, No. 17, Pater-noster Row.
[Price One Shilling.]

There are no cookery recipes. The cook maid is advised to buy The Complete English Cook, written by Mrs. Brookes.

1766 THE ART OF MODERN COOKERY DISPLAYED.

This book is given in Watt, but no copy has been seen of late years.

1767 THE MODERN ART OF COOKERY IMPROVED:
or, Elegant, Cheap, and Easy Methods, of preparing most of the Dishes now in Vogue; in the Composition whereof both Health and Pleasure have been consulted.
By Mrs. Ann Shackleford, of Winchester.
To which is added an Appendix; containing a Dissertation on the different kinds of Food, their Nature, Quality, and various Uses, by a Physician.
And a Marketing Manual, and other useful Particulars by the Editor.

> She turns, on hospitable thoughts intent,
> What choice to chuse for delicacy best;
> What order, so contriv'd as not to mix
> Tastes, not well join'd, inelegant, but bring
> Taste after Taste, upheld with kindliest Change.
>   MILTON.

London, printed for J. Newberry, at the Bull and Sun, in St. Paul's Church-Yard; and F. Newberry, in Pater-noster-Row. 1767.

An undated edition was published in Dublin.

1767 THE COMPLETE ENGLISH COOK;
or, Prudent Housewife, being an entire new Collection of the most general, yet least expensive Receipts in every Branch of Cookery and Good Housewifery.

With Directions for

Roasting,	Fricaseys,	Potting,
Boiling,	Pies, Tarts,	Candying,
Stewing,	Puddings,	Collaring,
Ragoos,	Cheese-Cakes,	Pickling,
Soups,	Custards,	Preserving,
Sauces,	Jellies,	Made-Wines, &c.

Together with Directions for placing Dishes on Tables of Entertainment : And many other Things equally necessary. The Whole made easy to the meanest Capacity, and far more useful to young Beginners than any Book of the kind extant.

> In cooking Fowl, or Flesh, or Fish,
> Or any nice, or dainty Dish,
> With Care peruse this useful Book,
> 'Twill make you soon a perfect Cook.

By Ann Peckham of Leeds, who is well known to have been for Forty Years past one of the most noted Cooks in the County of York.

Leeds, printed by Griffith Wright, M DCC LXVII.

And Sold by the Author, and J. Ogle, in Leeds; and Messrs. Robinson and Roberts, in Pater-noster-Row, London.

<small>The second edition is 1771 ; the third, undated, contains a supplement.</small>

<small>It is strange that the title-page should have been taken bodily from The Complete English Cook of Catharine Brooks. It is purely a cookery book, with many tables of courses at the end.</small>

1767 THE YOUNG LADIES SCHOOL OF ARTS, containing a great Variety of Practical Receipts, in

Gum-Flowers	Cosmetics	Jamms
Filligree	Jellies	Pickles
Japanning	Preserves	Candying
Shell-Work	Cakes	Made Wines
Gilding	Cordials	Clear Starching, &c.
Painting	Creams	

ENGLISH COOKERY BOOKS

Also, a great many Curious Receipts both useful and entertaining, never before published.

By Mrs. Hannah Robertson.

The Second Edition, with large Additions.

Edinburgh, printed by Wal. Ruddiman Junior, for Mrs. Robertson: Sold by her, and by all the Booksellers in England and Scotland. M DCC LXVII.

<small>There is an engraved half-title. A fourth edition was published at York in 1777. The book is a duodecimo of 182 pages dedicated to a Mrs. Lockhart of Craighouse, Scotland, who seems to have been endowed with both external and internal beauty.</small>

1767 PRIMITIVE COOKERY:

or the Kitchen Garden display'd. Containing a Collection of Receipts for preparing a great Variety of cheap, healthful and palatable Dishes, without either Fish, Flesh, or Fowl; with a Bill of Fare of Seventy Dishes, that will not cost above Two-pence each.

Likewise Directions for pickling, gathering, and preserving Herbs, Fruits and Flowers;

With many other Articles appertaining to the Product of the Kitchen-Garden, Orchard, &c.

The Second Edition. With considerable Additions.

Be not amongst wine-bibbers, amongst riotous eaters of flesh: for the drunkard and the glutton shall come to poverty. Prov.

London, printed for J. Williams, at No. 38. Fleet-Street. 1767.
[Price One Shilling.]

<small>This is a book of vegetarian cookery. Few of the seventy dishes could now be obtained for twopence. The first consists of asparagus, butter, salt, and bread.</small>

1768 THE COMPLETE COOK:

teaching the Art of Cookery in All its Branches; and to Spread a Table, in a Useful, Substantial and Splendid Manner, at all Seasons in the Year.

With Practical Instructions to Choose, Buy, Dress and Carve all Sorts of Provisions.

Far exceeding any Thing of the Kind yet Published.

Containing the greatest Variety of Approved Receipts in

> Cookery, Preserving,
> Pastry, Pickling,
> Confectionary, Collaring, &c.

And Dishes for Lent and Fast-Days, a Variety of Made Dishes, and to Dress both the Real and Mock Turtle.

With an Appendix teaching the Art of Making Wine, Mead, Cyder, Shrub, Strong, Cordial and Medical Waters; Brewing Malt Liquor; the Management and Breeding of Poultry and Bees: and Receipts for Preserving and Restoring Health and Relieving Pain; and for Taking out Stains, Preserving Furniture, Cleaning Plate, &c.

For the Use of Families.

By James Jenks, Cook.

London, printed for E. and C. Dilly in the Poultry. M DCC LXVIII.

The medical receipts are few, and it requires faith to believe in remedies which are to be taken 'at the changes of the moon'. Snail-water is still the authorized cure for consumption.

1769 THE EXPERIENCED ENGLISH HOUSE-KEEPER,

for the Use and Ease of Ladies, House-keepers, Cooks, &c. Wrote purely from Practice, and dedicated to the Hon. Lady Elizabeth Warburton, whom the Author lately served as House-keeper.

Consisting of near 800 Original Receipts, most of which never appeared in Print.

Part First, Lemon Pickle, Browning for all Sorts of Made Dishes, Soups, Fish, plain Meat, Game, Made Dishes both hot and cold, Pyes, Puddings, &c.

Part Second, All Kind of Confectionary, particularly the

Gold and Silver Web for covering of Sweetmeats, and a Desert of Spun Sugar, with Directions to set out a Table in the most elegant Manner and in the modern Taste, Floating Islands, Fish Ponds, Transparent Puddings, Trifles, Whips, &c.
Part Third, Pickling, Potting, and Collaring, Wines, Vinegars, Catchups, Distilling, with two most valuable Receipts, one for refining Malt Liquors, the other for curing Acid Wines, and a correct List of every Thing in Season in every Month of the Year.
By Elizabeth Raffald.
Manchester, printed by J. Harrop, for the Author, and sold by Messrs. Fletcher and Anderson, in St. Paul's Church-Yard, London; and by Eliz. Raffald, Confectioner, near the Exchange, Manchester, 1769.
The Book to be signed by the Author's own Hand-writing, and entered at Stationers Hall.

Other editions are 1773 (3), 1775 (4), 1776 (5), 1778 (6), 1780 (7), 1782 (8), 1784 (9), 1786 (10), 1794 (11), 1799 (12), 1806 (13). Still others, mostly described as new, and some of which seem pirated editions, are 1787, 1788, 1791, 1793, 1794, 1795, 1796, 1798, 1803, 1805, 1814, 1825.

There is an engraving of the lady as frontispiece to most of the editions. The life of the authoress is given in Manchester Collectanea, vol. ii, published by the Chetham Society in 1867. She was a Miss Whitaker of Doncaster, married in 1763, kept first a confectioner's shop and then three inns in succession. She is said to have had sixteen daughters in eighteen years. In 1772, 1773, and 1781 she brought out a Manchester directory. In the latter year she died.

1769 THE ART OF COOKERY AND PASTERY made easy and familiar, in upwards of two hundred different Receipts and Bills of Fare, never before made public.
To which is added, a Variety of Tables for Forms of Entertainment, and an exact Representation of the Tables at the Guild-Feasts of Norwich and Lynn.

By J. Skeat, Cook.

London, printed for the Author and Sold by him at his House next Door to the Maid's Head, in St. Simon's; and by J. Crouse, at the Back of the Inns, Norwich.

Price Two Shillings and Six Pence.

This is a large quarto, the date of its entry at Stationers' Hall being given as June 19, 1769. Many of the recipes seem new, e.g. 'Beef Troublon', 'A Baragade', 'A Gondevon', &c. The tables at the end are most interesting.

1769 THE LADY'S, HOUSEWIFE'S, AND COOK-MAID'S ASSISTANT:

or, The Art of Cookery explained and adapted to the meanest Capacity.

Containing,

I. How to roast and boil to perfection every thing necessary to be sent up to table.
II. Of made-dishes.
III. To make a number of pretty little dishes for a supper or side-dish, and little corner dishes for a great table.
IV. To dress fish.
V. Of soups and broths.
VI. Of puddings.
VII. Of pies.
VIII. Of hogs puddings, sausages, &c.
IX. To pot and make hams, &c.
X. Of pickling.
XI. Of making cakes, &c.
XII. Of cheese cakes, creams, jellies, whip-syllabubs, &c.
XIII. Of made-wines, brewing, French bread, muffins, &c.
XIV. Jarring cherries, preserves.
XV. To dress turtle, and make mock turtle.

The whole designed to fit out an Entertainment in an Elegant Manner, and at a small Expense.

By E. Taylor.

Berwick upon Tweed, printed by H. Taylor, for R. Taylor, Bookseller. MDCCLXIX.

A duodecimo of 276 pages. There is a list of subscribers at the beginning.

1769 THE PROFESSED COOK :
or, The Modern Art of Cookery, Pastry, and Confectionary, made Plain and Easy. Consisting of the most approved Methods in the French as well as English Cookery. In which the French Names of all the different Dishes are given and explained, whereby every Bill of Fare becomes intelligible and familiar. Containing

I. Of Soups, Gravy, Cullis and Broths
II. Of Sauces
III. The different Ways of Dressing Beef, Veal, Mutton, Pork, Lamb, &c.
IV. Of First Course Dishes
V. Of Dressing Poultry
VI. Of Venison
VII. Of Game of all Sorts
VIII. Of Ragouts, Collops and Fries
IX. Of Dressing all Kinds of Fish
X. Of Pastry of different Kinds
XI. Of Entremets, or Last Course Dishes
XII. Of Omelets
XIII. Pastes of different Sorts
XIV. Dried Conserves
XV. Cakes, Wafers and Biscuits
XVI. Of Almonds and Pistachias made in different Ways
XVII. Marmalades
XVIII. Jellies
XIX. Liquid and Dried Sweetmeats
XX. Syrups and Brandy Fruits
XXI. Ices, Ice Creams and Ice Fruits
XXII. Ratifias, and other Cordials, &c. &c.

Translated from Les Soupers de la Cour, with the Addition of the best Receipts which have ever appear'd in the French Language.

And adapted to the London Markets by the Editor, who has been many Years Clerk of the Kitchen in some of the first Families in this Kingdom.

The Second Edition.

London, printed for A. Davis, in Piccadilly; and T. Caslon, opposite Stationers Hall. M DCC LXIX.

Later editions, 1776 (3), 1812 (10), give the name of the author as B. Clermont. The 1769 edition in the B. M. is catalogued under the word 'Soupers'. The French original (1755) is by Menon, author of other cookery books.

102 ENGLISH COOKERY BOOKS

1770 THE COURT AND COUNTRY CONFECTIONER: or, The House-Keeper's Guide; to a more speedy, plain, and familiar method of understanding the whole art of confectionary, pastry, distilling, and the making of fine flavoured English wines from all kinds of fruits, herbs, and flowers; comprehending near four hundred and fifty easy and practical receipts, never before made known.

Particularly,

Preserving.	Puff, Spun, and Fruit-Pastes.
Candying.	Light-Biscuits.
Icing.	Puffs.
Transparent marmalade,	Rich Seed-Cakes.
Orange,	Custards.
Pine-Apple,	Syllabubs.
Pistachis, and other Rich Creams.	Flummeries.
	Trifles, Whips, Fruits, and other Jellies.
Caramel.	Pickles, &c. &c.
Pastils.	
Bomboons.	

Also new and easy directions for clarifying the different degrees of sugar, together with several bills of fare of deserts for private gentlemen's families.

To which is added a dissertation on the different species of fruits, and the art of distilling simple waters, cordials, perfumed oils, and essences.

By an Ingenious Foreigner, now head confectioner to the Spanish Ambassador in England.

London, printed for G. Riley, and A. Cooke, at their Circulating Library, Queen Street, Berkeley Square; J. Bell, near Exeter-Exchange, in the Strand; J. Wheble, at No. 20, Pater-noster-row; and C. Etherington, at York. M DCC LXX.

A new edition, 1772, gives the author's name as Borella. It is a well-arranged book of 271 pages with 46 additional pages on distilling.

1770 (c.) THE NEW LONDON AND COUNTRY COOK, or, The Whole Art of Cookery Displayed in the Newest and Most Fashionable Taste. Being a Complete Collection of Receipts, by the Knowledge of which a Table may be handsomely set out with the choicest Dishes, in the genteelest Manner, and with greatest Oeconomy. The Directions for which are under the following Heads, viz.,

Boiling,	Gravies,	Puddings,
Roasting,	Sauces,	Jellies,
Frying,	Made Dishes,	Creams,
Broiling,	Potting,	Candies,
Stewing,	Collaring,	Syrups,
Hashing,	Pies,	Pickling,
Soups,	Tarts,	and
Broths,	Cakes,	Preserving.

Also the whole Art of Clear Starching, together with other important Matters.

The Whole being so plain that every Capacity may comprehend the Instructions with Ease; the most ignorant put them in Practice with Pleasure, and those least acquainted with Cookery, become, in a short Time, complete Cooks without any other Instructions.

By Caroline Butler, of Charlotte-Street, who has practised Cookery in all its various Branches, and in the best Families, upwards of Thirty Years.

> Her plain Directions you may see
> To roast, boil, fry, or fricassee:
> To make, with Nicety and Ease,
> What will the daintiest Palate please:
> That when each sav'ry Dish is dress'd,
> You'll be allow'd a Cook Profess'd.

London, printed for J. Cooke, No. 17, Pater-noster Row.
[Price One Shilling.]

A pamphlet of 108 pages. There is a frontispiece representing a kitchen with the lines:

> If in the Modern Taste, you'd learn to Cook,
> Study the Perfect Method in our Book.
> Then the Best Table you may serve with Ease,
> And the Nice Appetite exactly Please.

104 ENGLISH COOKERY BOOKS

1770 (*c.*) THE LADIES DELIGHT :
or Cook-Maids best Instructor.
London, printed for Henry Woodgate, and Samuel Brooks, at the Golden Ball, in Pater-noster-Row.

This little book of 116 pages has unfortunately lost its title-page. At the end is a catalogue of 'Chapmens Books'.

1770 (*c.*) THE BRITISH HOUSEWIFE :
or, the Cook, Housekeeper's, and Gardiner's Companion.
Calculated for the Service both of London and the Country ; And directing what is to be done in the Providing for, Conducting, and Managing a Family throughout the Year.
Containing a general Account of fresh Provisions of all Kinds. Of the several foreign Articles for the Table, pickled, or otherwise preserved ; and the different Kinds of Spices, Salts, Sugars, and other Ingredients used in Pickling and Preserving at Home : Shewing what each is, whence it is brought, and what are its Qualities and Uses.
Together with the Nature of all Kinds of Foods, and the Method of suiting them to different Constitutions ;
A Bill of Fare for each Month, the Art of Marketing and chusing fresh Provisions of all Kinds ; and the making as well as chusing of Hams, Tongues, and other Store Dishes.
Also Directions for plain Roasting and Boiling ; and for the Dressing of all Sorts of Made Dishes in various Tastes ; and the preparing the Desert in all its Articles.
Containing a greater Variety than was ever before publish'd, of the most Elegant, yet least Expensive Receipts in

Cookery,	Fricassees,	Tarts,	Dry'd Fruits,
Pastry,	Ragouts,	Cakes,	Sweetmeats,
Puddings,	Soups,	Creams,	Made Wines,
Preserves,	Sauces,	Custards,	Cordials, and
Pickles,	Jellies,	Candies,	Distillery.

To which are annexed,
The Art of Carving ; and the Terms used for cutting up

various Things; and the polite and easy Manner of doing the Honours of the Table: The whole Practice of Pickling and Preserving: And of preparing made Wines, Beer, and Cyder. As also of distilling all the useful Kinds of Cordial and Simple Waters.

With the Conduct of a Family in Respect of Health ; the Disorders to which they are every Month liable, and the most approved Remedies for each.

And a Variety of other valuable Particulars, necessary to be known in All Families ; and nothing inserted but what has been approved by Experience.

Also the Ordering of all Kinds of profitable Beasts and Fowls, with respect to their Choice, their Breeding and Feeding ; the Diseases to which they are severally liable each Month, and Receipts for their Cure. Together with the Management of the pleasure, profitable, and useful Garden. The whole embellished with a great Number of curious Copper Plates, shewing the Manner of Trussing all Kinds of Game, wild and tame Fowls, &c., as also the Order of setting out Tables for Dinners, Suppers, and Grand Entertainments, in a Method never before attempted ; and by which even those who cannot read will be able to instruct themselves.

By Mrs. Martha Bradley, late of Bath : being the Result of upwards of Thirty Years Experience.

The whole (which is deduc'd from Practice) compleating the careful Reader, from the highest to the lowest Degree, in every Article of English Housewifery.

London, printed for S. Crowder and H. Woodgate, at the Golden Ball in Paternoster Row.

This is a book of 752 pages bound in two volumes. There is a frontispiece representing a kitchen with the lettering :

> Behold, ye Fair, united in this Book,
> The frugal Housewife, and experienced Cook.

Powdered earthworms are still recommended for the ague.

1773 COOKERY AND PASTRY.
As taught and practised by Mrs. Maciver, teacher of those Arts in Edinburgh.
Edinburgh, printed for the Author; and sold by her, at her house, Stephen Law's close, back of the City-guard. M DCC LXXIII.

Other editions are 1777 (2), 1782 (3), 1784 (4), 1789, 1800.

1772 THE COMPLETE HOUSE-KEEPER, AND PROFESSED COOK,
calculated for the greater Ease and Assistance of Ladies, House-keepers, Cooks, &c. &c.
Containing upwards of Seven Hundred practical and approved Receipts, arranged under the following Heads:

I. Rules for Marketing
II. Boiling, Roasting, and Broiling Flesh, Fish, and Fowls; and for making Soups and Sauces of all Kinds.
III. Making made Dishes of all Sorts, Puddings, Pies, Cakes, Fritters, &c.
IV. Pickling, Preserving, and making Wines in the best Manner and Taste.
V. Potting and Collaring; Aspikes in Jellies; savoury Cakes, Blamonge, Ice Creams and other Creams, Whips, Jellies, &c.
VI. Bills of Fare for every Month in the Year; with a correct List of every Thing in Season for every Month; illustrated with two elegant Copper-plates of a First and Second Course for a genteel Table.

A New Edition, with considerable Additions and Improvements.
By Mary Smith, late House-Keeper to Sir Walter Blackett, Bart. and formerly in the Service of the Right Hon. Lord Anson, Sir Thomas Sebright, Bart. and other Families of Distinction, as House-keeper and Cook.
Newcastle, printed for S. Hodgson; and G. G. J. and J. Robinson, Paternoster Row, London. M DCC LXXXVI.

According to Ellwanger the first edition was 1772.

ENGLISH COOKERY BOOKS

1774 A COLLECTION OF ONE HUNDRED AND THIRTY-SEVEN APPROVED RECEIPTS

in Pastry and Cookery,

viz.

Bread,
Pastes,
Baken Meats,
Seed Cakes,
Preserves,
Marmalades,
Jellies,

Confections,
Rules for a Cook-Maid,
Dressing of Meat in different Ways,
Fattening Fowls,
Carving, &c. &c.

To which are added, Directions for making the best Cosmetics, Washing Gauges, Muslins, &c. and Painting of Rooms, Stair Cases, &c.

Aberdeen, printed for Alexander Thomson, Bookseller in the Castlegate. M DCC LXXIV.

A small duodecimo of 52 pages. There is a half-title before the title-page.

1775 (c.) A CHOICE COLLECTION OF COOKERY RECEIPTS.

Newcastle, printed in this present Year.

A chap-book of 24 pages with a rude frontispiece. An abbreviated edition was published at Stirling by C. Randall in 1801. It has a different frontispiece.

1775 THE LADY'S ASSISTANT

for Regulating and Supplying her Table, being a Complete System of Cookery, containing one Hundred and Fifty select Bills of Fare, properly disposed for Family Dinners of Five Dishes, to Two Courses of Eleven and Fifteen;

With upwards of Fifty Bills of Fare for Suppers, from Five Dishes to Nineteen; and several Deserts:

Including likewise, the fullest and choicest Receipts of various Kinds, with full Directions for preparing them in the most approved Manner, from which a continual Change may be made, as wanted, in the several Bills of Fare:

Published from the Manuscript Collection of Mrs. Charlotte

Mason, a Professed Housekeeper, who had upwards of Thirty Years Experience in Families of the first Fashion.
The Second Edition corrected, and considerably enlarged.
" The most refin'd understanding and the most exalted sentiments do not place a woman above the little duties of life." MRS. GRIFFITH.
London, printed for J. Walter, at Homer's-Head, Charing-Cross. M DCC LXXV.

There is a half-title. Other editions are 1777 (3), 1786 (new), 1793 (7). It seems an excellent and well-arranged book, but few people now would care for ' Viper Broth '.

1775 VALUABLE SECRETS CONCERNING ARTS AND TRADES:
or approved Directions from the best Artists . . .
Hic tibi erunt Artes! VIRG.
London; printed and sold by Will. Hay, Printer and Bookseller to the Society of Artists of Great Britain, at his Shop next Door to their Exhibition-hall, near Exeter 'Change, Strand. M DCC LXXV.

Chapter 14 gives the art of confectionary.

1777 THE YOUNG LADIES' GUIDE
in the Art of Cookery: being a Collection of useful Receipts, published for the Convenience of the Ladies committed to her Care.
By Eliz. Marshall.
Newcastle; printed by T. Saint, for the Author. M DCC LXXVII.

The preface is addressed ' to the Young Ladies who have done me the Honour of attending my School '.

1780 A FORME OF CURY,
a Roll of Ancient English Cookery, compiled, about A.D. 1390, by the Master-Cooks of King Richard II, presented afterwards to Queen Elizabeth, by Edward Lord Stafford, and now in the Possession of Gustavus Brander, Esq.
Illustrated with Notes, and a copious Index, or Glossary.

A Manuscript of the Editor, of the same Age and Subject, is subjoined.

By an Antiquary.

" — ingeniosa gula est." MARTIAL.

London, printed by J. Nicholls. M DCC LXXX.

The editor was Samuel Pegge.

1780 (*c.*) THE NEW BOOK OF COOKERY; or every Woman a perfect Cook; containing the greatest Variety of approved Receipts in all the Branches of Cookery and Confectionary, viz.,

Boiling,	Made-Dishes,	Jellies,
Roasting,	Soups and Sauces,	Pickling,
Broiling,	Puddings,	Preserving,
Frying,	Pies and Tarts,	Candying,
Stewing,	Cakes,	Drying,
Hashing,	Custards,	Potting,
Baking,	Cheesecakes,	Collaring,
Fricassees,	Creams,	English Wines,
Ragouts,	Syllabubs,	&c. &c. &c.

To which are added, the best instructions for Marketing, and sundry modern Bills of Fare; also Directions for Clear Starching, and the Ladies' Toilet, or, Art of preserving and improving Beauty; likewise a Collection of Physical Receipts for Families, &c.

The Whole calculated to assist the prudent Housewife and her Servants, in furnishing the cheapest and most elegant Set of Dishes in the various Departments of Cookery, and to instruct Ladies in many other Particulars of Great Importance too numerous to mention in the Title Page.

By Mrs. Eliz. Price, of Berkeley Square, assisted by others who have made the Art of Cookery their constant Study.

A new edition for the present year, with great Additions.

> Here you may quickly learn with Care,
> To act the Housewife's Part,
> And dress a modern Bill of Fare
> With Elegance and Art.

London, printed for the Authoress, and sold by Alex. Hogg, No. 16, Pater-Noster-Row.

(Price only One Shilling.)

1780 (c.) THE NEW, UNIVERSAL, AND COMPLETE CONFECTIONER;

or the whole art of confectionary made perfectly plain and easy. Containing full Accounts of all the various Methods of Preserving and Candying, both dry and liquid, Fruit, Flowers, Garden Stuff, Herbs, &c.

Also the several Ways of clarifying Sugar; and the best Methods of keeping Fruit, Nuts, and Flowers, Fresh and Fine all the Year round:

Together with Directions for Making

Blomonge,	Jellies,	Syrups of all Kinds,
Biscuits,	Creams,	Jams,
Cakes,	Ices,	Conserves,
Rock-Works,	Whip Syllabubs,	Cordials,
Candies,	Cheesecakes,	Compotes,
Tarts,	Sweetmeats,	Knicknacks,
Possets,	Puffs & Pastes,	Trifles, Comfits,
Custards,	Oils, &c.	Drops, &c. &c. &c.

Including various Modern and Original Receipts for making Lemonade, Orgeat, Orangeade, Waters, and other Refreshments.

By Mrs. Elizabeth Price, of Berkeley Square, Author of The New Book of Cookery. Embellished with an Elegant Frontispiece.

London, printed for Alex. Hogg, No. 16, Paternoster-Row, by S. Couchman, Throgmorton-Street.

[Price only 1s. 6d.]

This is a small book of 94 pages. There is a frontispiece of a lady giving a book to her cook.

The whole Art of Confectionary, by Mrs. Eliz. Glasse, with no publisher's name and a preface signed Elizabeth Price, but copied from H. Glasse, seems another edition issued for fraudulent purposes. It is, however, a much larger book.

ENGLISH COOKERY BOOKS

1780 (c.) THE NEW AND COMPLETE UNIVERSAL COOK;

or, Young Woman's Best Guide, in the whole Art of Cookery. Giving particular Directions for Boiling, Roasting, Frying, Broiling, and Stewing; and the most approved Methods of making Hashes, Gravies, Sauces, Soups, Fricassees, &c.

Together with the whole Art of Pastry; and the choicest Receipts for Cakes, &c. &c.

To which are added many other Particulars.

By Mrs. Ann Partridge, of Great George-Street, Westminster.

London, printed for Alex. Hogg, at No. 16, Paternoster-Row, and sold by all other Booksellers.

[Price only Six-Pence, with a Frontispiece.]

The frontispiece is the same as that to The New, Universal, and Complete Confectioner of Elizabeth Price, with the lettering:

The cheapest Present for a Servant Maid.

The Housewife fair this Book has read,
And now presents it to her Maid,
Th' Universal Cook does here impart,
That she may fully Learn the Art.

It is a little book of 70 pages.

1780 (c.) THE FARMER'S WIFE;

or, Complete Country Housewife. Containing

Full and ample Directions for the Breeding and Management of Turkies, Fowls, Geese, Ducks, Pigeons, &c.

Instructions for fattening Hogs, pickling of Pork, and curing of Bacon.

How to make Sausages, Hogs-Puddings, &c.

Full Instructions for making Wines from various Kinds of English Fruits, and from Smyrna Raisins.

The Method of making Cyder, Perry, Mead, Mum, Cherry-Brandy, &c.

Directions respecting the Dairy, containing the best Way of making Butter, and likewise Gloucestershire, Cheshire, Stilton, Sage, and Cream Cheese.

How to pickle common English Fruits and Vegetables, with other useful Receipts for the Farmer's Wife and Country House-Keeper.

Full Instructions how to brew Beer and Ale, of all the various Kinds made in this Kingdom.

Ample Directions respecting the Management of Bees, with an account of the Use of Honey.

To which is added the Art of Breeding and Managing Song Birds in General ; likewise a Variety of Receipts in Cookery. And other Particulars well worthy the Attention of Women of all Ranks residing in the Country.

> Instructions, full and plain, we give,
> To teach the Farmer's Wife,
> With Satisfaction how to live
> The happy Country Life.

London, printed for Alex. Hogg, No. 16, in Pater-noster Row.
[Price One Shilling and Six-pence.]

A small book of 132 pages with a frontispiece representing a farmyard.

1780 (c.) The ACCOMPLISHED LADY'S DELIGHT IN COOKERY ;

or The Complete Servant's-Maid's Guide.

Wolverhampton, printed by J. Smart.

A pamphlet of 24 pages with two rude cuts on the title-page.

1780 (c.) THE BRITISH JEWEL,

or, Complete Housewife's Best Companion ; containing,

I. A number of the most uncommon and useful Receipts in Cookery, with the Manner of Trussing Poultry, Rabbits, Hares, &c. illustrated with curious Cuts, shewing how each is to be trussed.

II. The best and most fashionable Receipts for all Manner of Pastry, Pickling, &c. with some general Rules to be observed therein.

III. Directions for making all Sorts of English Wines, Shrub, Vinegar, Verjuice, Catchup, Sauces, Soups, Jellies, &c.

IV. A Table to cast up

Expences by the Day, Week, Month, or Year.

V. Every Man his own Physician ; a valuable Collection of the most approved Receipts for the Cure of most Disorders incident to human Bodies, from the most eminent English Physician.

VI. The Manner of preparing the Elixir of Life, Turlington's Balsam, Fryar's Balsam, the Court or Lady's Black Sticking Plaster, Lip-Salve, Lady York's Receipt to preserve from the Small-Pox or Plague, &c. the Royal Patent Snuff for the Head and Eyes ; Dr. Braken's Powder for the Teeth, a Secret for the Cure of the Tooth-ach, a speedy Method to destroy Warts or Corns, &c.

VII. Directions for destroying Rats, Mice, Bugs, Fleas, &c.

And a choice Variety of Useful Family Receipts, together with a Method of restoring to Life People drowned, or in any other Manner suffocated. Also the Complete Farrier, being the Method of Bying, Selling, Managing, &c. and of the Diseases incident to Horses, with their Cures.

To which is added The Royal Gardener, or Monthly Calendar.

London, printed and sold by J. Miller, No. 14, White-lion-street, Goodman's-Fields. Price, One Shilling.

A pamphlet of 104 pages. A new edition (1782) has a rude frontispiece representing the Good Samaritan and a kitchen.

1781 THE PRACTICE OF MODERN COOKERY ;
adapted to Families of Distinction, as well as to those of the Middling Ranks of Life.

To which is added a Glossary explaining the Terms of Art.

By George Dalrymple, late Cook to Sir John Whitefoord, Bart.

Edinburgh, printed for the Author. Sold by C. Elliot, Edinburgh ; and T. Longman, London. M DCC LXXXI.

There is a half-title before the title-page. A book of 475 pages, dedicated to Lady Whitefoord.

1783 THE LONDON ART OF COOKERY,
and Housekeeper's Complete Assistant, on a new plan made Plain and Easy to the Understanding of every Housekeeper, Cook, and Servant in the Kingdom.
Containing,

- Proper Directions for the Choice of all Kinds of Provisions.
- Roasting and Boiling all Sorts of Butchers Meat, Poultry, Game, and Fish.
- Sauces for every Occasion.
- Soups, Broths, Stews, and Hashes.
- Made Dishes, Ragoos, and Fricassees.
- All Sorts of Pies and Puddings.
- Proper Instructions for dressing Fruits and Vegetables.
- Pickling, Potting, and Preserving.
- The Preparation of Hams, Tongues, and Bacon.
- The whole Art of Confectionary.
- Tarts, Puffs, and Pasties.
- Cakes, Custards, Jams, and Jellies.
- Drying, Candying, and Preserving Fruits, &c.
- Made Wines, Cordial Waters, and Malt Liquors.

To which is added an Appendix, containing Considerations on Culinary Poisons; Directions for making Broths, &c. for the Sick; a List of Things in Season in the different Months of the Year; Marketing Tables, &c. &c.

Embellished with a Head of the Author, and a Bill of Fare for every Month in the Year, elegantly engraved on Thirteen Copper-plates.

By John Farley, principal cook at the London Tavern.

London, printed for John Fielding, No. 23, Pater-noster Row; and J. Scatcherd and J. Whitaker, No. 12, Ave Maria Lane, 1783.

[Price Six Shillings Bound.]

Other editions are 1784 (2), 1785 (3), 1787 (4), 1789 (6), 1792 (7), 1796 (8), 1800 (9), 1804 (10), 1807 (11), 1811 (12). The author claims that his work, unlike so many which are without method or order, is marked by ' Perspicuity and Regularity '.

1783 THE HOUSE-KEEPER'S POCKET BOOK,
and Compleat Family Cook, containing several hundred curious receipts in

>   Cookery,   Brewing,
>   Pastry,   Baking,
>   Preserving,   Made Wines, &c.
>   Pickling,

With plain and easy instructions for preparing and dressing every thing suitable for an elegant Entertainment, from Two Dishes to Five or Ten, &c. To which is Added,
Every Man his own Doctor, shewing the Nature and Faculties of the different sorts of Foods, whereby every Man and Woman may know what is Good or Hurtful to them.
Printed by Thomas Martin No. 76 Wood-street Cheapside.

A small book of 168 pages. A rude frontispiece has the lettering, 'Engraved for Mrs. Harrisons Cookery Book 1785,' but the book is quite different from Mrs. Harrison's book of the same title.

1788 THE ENGLISH ART OF COOKERY,
according to the Present Practice; being a Complete Guide to all Housekeepers, on a plan entirely new; consisting of thirty-eight chapters. Containing,

Proper Directions for Marketing, and Trussing of Poultry,
The making of Soups and Broths,
Dressing all Sorts of Fish,
Sauces for every Occasion,
Boiling and Roasting,
Baking, Broiling, and Frying,
Stews and Hashes,
Made Dishes of every Sort,
Ragous and Fricasees,
Directions for dressing all
Sorts of Roots and Vegetables,
All Sorts of Aumlets and Eggs,
Puddings, Pies, Tarts, &c.
Pancakes and Fritters,
Cheesecakes and Custards,
Blancmange, Jellies, and Syllabubs,
Directions for the Sick,
Directions for Seafaring Men,
Preserving, Syrups, and Conserves,
Drying and Candying,

116   ENGLISH COOKERY BOOKS

All Sorts of Cakes,
Hogs Puddings, Sausages, &c.
Potting, and little cold Dishes,
The Art of Carving,
Collaring, Salting, and Sousing,
Pickling,
To keep Garden Vegetables, &c.
A Catalogue of Things in Season,
Made Wines and Cordial Waters,
Brewing,
English and French Bread, &c.

With Bills of Fare for every month in the year.
Neatly and correctly engraved on Twelve Copper-Plates.
The Third Edition.
By Richard Briggs, many years Cook at the White-Hart Tavern, Holborn, Temple Coffee-House, and other Taverns in London.
London, printed for G. G. and J. Robinson, Pater-Noster-Row. M DCC XCIV.

Watt gives the first edition as 1788. The second was 1791. An edition called 'The New Art of Cookery' was published at Philadelphia in 1792.

1788 THE HONOURS OF THE TABLE,
or, Rules for behaviour during meals; with the whole Art of Carving, illustrated by a variety of cuts.
Together with Directions for going to Market, and the Method of distinguishing good Provisions from bad; to which is added a Number of Hints or concise Lessons for the Improvement of Youth, on all occasions in Life.
By the Author of Principles of Politeness, &c.
"To do the honours of a table gracefully, is one of the outlines of a well-bred man; and to carve well, little as it may seem, is useful twice every day, and the doing of which ill is not only troublesome to ourselves, but renders us disagreeable and ridiculous to others." LORD CHESTERFIELD'S LETTERS.
For the use of young people.
London, printed for the Author, at the Literary-Press,

No. 14, Red-Lion-Street, Clerkenwell; and may be had of H. D. Symmonds, Paternoster-Row, and all Book-sellers in Town and Country, M DCC LXXXVIII.

By J. Trusler. Other editions are 1791 (2) and 1801 (3). The fourth and fifth editions are undated. The book gives curious information as to the habits of the time. For example, the custom of 'a gentleman and a lady sitting alternately round the table' had only been lately introduced. Till then the ladies had sat together according to rank. 'Habit has made a pint of wine after dinner almost necessary to a man who eats freely.'

1789 THE COMPLETE CONFECTIONER;
or, the Whole Art of Confectionary: forming a Ready Assistant to all Genteel Families; giving them a Perfect Knowledge of Confectionary; with Instructions, neatly engraved on ten copper-plates, how to decorate a Table with Taste and Elegance, without the Expense or Assistance of a Confectioner.
By a Person, late an Apprentice to the well-known Messrs Negri and Witten, of Berkeley-Square.
London: printed for the Author; and sold by J. Matthews, No. 18, Strand, M DCC LXXXIX.
[Price 10s. 6d. neatly bound.]
Entered at Stationers Hall.

By Frederick Nutt. There is a half-title before the title-page. A preliminary note says that the original title was altered in consequence of the author having found that it had been used by Mrs. Glass.

Other editions are 1790 (2), 1806 (3), 1807 (4), 1809 (6), 1815 (7), 1819 (8).

1789 A new edition improved, with a list of every thing in season, several bills of fare, and an elegant collection of light dishes for supper.

THE LADY'S COMPLETE GUIDE;
or Cookery and Confectionary in all their Branches. Containing the most approved Receipts, confirmed by

Observation and Practice, in every reputable English Book of Cookery now extant; besides a great Variety of others which have never before been offered to the Public. Also several translated from the Productions of Cooks of Eminence who have published in France, particularly the Duke de Nivernois, M. Comms's *Histoire de Cuisine*, M. Disang's *Maitre d'Hotel*, M. Valois, and M. Delatour, with their respective Names to each Receipt; which, with the Original Articles, form the most complete System of Cookery ever yet exhibited, under the following Heads, viz.

Roasting,	Soups,	Tarts,
Boiling,	Sauces,	Pies,
Made-Dishes,	Gravies,	Pasties,
Frying,	Hashes,	Cheesecakes,
Broiling,	Stews,	Jellies,
Potting,	Puddings,	Pickling,
Fricassees,	Custards,	Preserving,
Ragouts,	Cakes,	Confectionary, &c.

To which is added, in order to render it as complete and perfect as possible, the Complete Brewer; containing familiar Instructions for brewing all Sorts of Beer and Ale; including the proper Management of the Vault or Cellar.

Also the Family Physician; consisting of a considerable Collection of approved Prescriptions by Mead, Sydenham, Tissot, Fothergill, Elliot, Buchan, and Others, including a certain Remedy for that formidable Disorder, the Dropsy, recommended by Persons respectable in the highest Degree. By Mrs. Mary Cole, cook to the Right Hon. the Earl of Drogheda.

London: printed for G. Kearsley, No. 46, Fleet-Street, 1789.

[Price 6s. in boards, or 7s, bound.]

This is a large book of 564 pages. It is strange that none of the French books mentioned on the title-page seem to be in Vicaire, and some other French writers, who are mentioned in the preface, are not to be found there. There is an edition of 1791 (3). The author prides herself on giving references to former books of cookery whenever she quotes, and even specifying the pages where the several receipts can be found. The preface states that the first edition was sold out in six weeks.

1790 THE LADIES' LIBRARY:
or, Encyclopædia of Female Knowledge, in every Branch of Domestic Economy : comprehending, in alphabetical arrangement, Distinct Treatises on every Practical Subject, necessary for Servants and Mistresses of Families.

I. A most extensive System of Cookery.
II. A complete Body of Domestic Medicine.
III. The Preservation of Beauty, and Prevention of Deformity.

In which is included a Vast Fund of Miscellaneous Information, of the highest Importance in Domestic Life.

In Two Volumes.
Vol. I.

London, printed for J. Ridgway, No. 1, York Street, St. James's Square. M DCC XC.

As frontispiece there is a portrait of John Perkins, a cook whose Manuscript Recipes the editors have largely used. There is much curious information with respect to the domestic medicine and surgery of the day. 'Bleeding is often practised by midwives, gardeners, and blacksmiths; and the country barber generally takes the superintendance of the teeth.' There is a long article on inoculation for the small-pox. The fullest details are given on the assumption, apparently, that the lady of the house is to inoculate her family.

1790 A COLLECTION OF ORDINANCES AND REGULATIONS
for the Government of the Royal Household, made in divers reigns, from King Edward iii. to King William and Queen Mary. Also Receipts in Ancient Cookery.
London, printed for the Society of Antiquaries by John Nichols: sold by Messieurs White and Son; Robson; Leigh and Sotheby; Browne; and Egerton's. M DCC XC.

A large quarto of 466 pages.

1791 THE PRACTICE OF COOKERY, PASTRY, PICKLING, PRESERVING, &c.

Containing Figures of Dinners, from Five to Nineteen dishes, and a Full List of Supper Dishes : also a List of Things in Season, for every month in the Year, and Directions for choosing Provisions :

With Two Plates, showing the method of placing Dishes upon a Table, and the manner of Trussing Poultry, &c.

By Mrs. Frazer, Sole Teacher of these Arts in Edinburgh, several years Colleague, and afterwards Successor to Mrs. McIver deceased.

Edinburgh, printed for Peter Hill, Edinburgh, and T. Cadell, London. M,DCC,XCI.

Other editions are 1795 (2), 1800 (3), 1806 (5), 1820. The book is based on Mrs. Maciver's Cookery and Pastry.

1791 ANTIQUITATES CULINARIÆ ;

or Curious Tracts relating to the Culinary affairs of the Old English, with a preliminary discourse, Notes, and Illustrations,

By the Reverend Richard Warner, of Sway, near Lymington, Hants.

>Πολλῷ τόι πλέονας λίμοῦ κόρος ὤλεσεν ανδρασ
>
>Non in Caro nidore voluptas
>Summa, sed in teipso est ; tu pulmentaria quære
>Sudando.

London, printed for R. Blamire, Strand. 1791.

1792 THE UNIVERSAL COOK,

and City and Country Housekeeper, containing all the Various Branches of Cookery : the Different Methods of Dressing Butchers Meat, Poultry, Game, and Fish ; and of preparing Gravies, Cullices, Soups, and Broths ; to dress Roots and Vegetables, and to prepare little elegant Dishes for Suppers or light Repasts : to make all Sorts of Pies,

Puddings, Pancakes, and Fritters ; Cakes, Puffs, and Biscuits ; Cheesecakes, Tarts, and Custards ; Creams and Jams ; Blancmange, Flummery, Elegant Ornaments, Jellies, and Syllabubs. The various Articles in Candying, Drying, Preserving, and Pickling. The Preparation of Hams, Tongues, Bacon, &c. Directions for Trussing Poultry, Carving, and Marketing. The Making and Management of Made Wines, Cordial Waters, and Malt Liquors. Together with Directions for Baking Bread, the Management of Poultry and the Dairy, and the Kitchen and Fruit Garden ; with a Catalogue of the various Articles in Season in the different Months of the Year. Besides a Variety of Useful and Interesting Tables.

The Whole Embellished with the Heads of the Authors, Bills of Fare for every Month in the Year, and proper Subjects for the Improvement of the Art of Carving, elegantly engraved on fourteen Copper-plates.

By Francis Collingwood, and John Woollams, Principal Cooks at the Crown and Anchor Tavern in the Strand, Late from the London Tavern.

London, printed by R. Noble, for J. Scatcherd and J. Whitaker, No. 12, Ave-Maria-Lane. 1792.

Other editions are 1797 (2), 1806 (4), 1807 (also 4). There are portraits of the two authors as frontispiece. In the preface attention is called ' to the elegantly printing of the work ; a bare inspection into which will give it, in point of elegance, a decided superiority over every other book of the kind '. The book received the honour in 1810 of being translated into French.

1793 THE FRENCH FAMILY COOK :
being a complete System of French Cookery.
Adapted to the Tables not only of the Opulent, but of Persons of moderate Fortune and Condition. Containing Directions for Choosing, dressing, and serving up all Sorts of Butcher Meat, Poultry, &c.
The different Modes of making all kinds of Soups, Ragouts,

Fricandeaus, Creams, Ratafias, Compôts, Preserves, &c. &c. —as well as a great Variety of cheap and elegant Side Dishes, calculated to grace a Table at a small Expense.

Instructions for making out Bills of Fare for the four Seasons of the Year, and to furnish a Table with few or any number of Dishes at the most moderate possible Expense.

Necessary for Housekeepers, Butlers, Cooks, and all who are concerned in the Superintendence of a Family.

Translated from the French.

London, printed for J. Bell, No. 148, Oxford Street, nearly opposite New Bond Street. M DCC XCIII.

A book of 342 pages.

1794 DOMESTIC ECONOMY:
or, A Complete System of English Housekeeping.
By Maximilian Hazlemore.
London, printed for J. Creswick, and Co. 1794.

The whole of the title-page is not given, as it is almost identical with that of 'The Lady's Complete Guide' by Mrs. Mary Cole. The contents of the book are also identical, and one wonders who was the real author.

1795 THE FRUGAL HOUSEWIFE,
or, Complete Woman Cook, Wherein the Art of dressing all Sorts of Viands with Cleanliness, Decency and Elegance, is explained in Five Hundred Approved Receipts in Gravies, Sauces, Roasting, Boiling, Frying, Broiling, Stews, Hashes, Soups, Fricassees, Ragouts, Pastries, Pies, Tarts, Cakes, Puddings, Syllabubs, Creams, Flummery, Jellies, Giams, and Custards.

Together with the Best Methods of Potting, Collaring, Preserving, Drying, Candying, Pickling, and Making of English Wines; To which are added Twelve New Prints, exhibiting a proper Arrangement of Dinners, Two Courses for every Month in the Year, with various Bills of Fare.

By Susannah Carter, of Clerkenwell.

London, printed for E. Newbery, the corner of St. Paul's Church-Yard. 1795.

From the preface it seems that this is a 'revised and corrected Edition'. It is a small book of 192 pages. The first edition, undated, consists of 168 pages. An edition, later than 1795, is also undated. An edition, called 'The Frugal Housewife or Experienced Cook', appeared in 1823, 'originally written by Susanna Carter, but now improved by an experienced Cook in one of the Principal Taverns in the City of London.'

1795 THE NEW EXPERIENCED ENGLISH-HOUSE-KEEPER,

for the Use and Ease of Ladies, Housekeepers, Cooks, &c. written purely from her own practice.

By Mrs. Sarah Martin, many years Housekeeper to the late Freeman Bower Esq. of Bawtry.

Being an entire new Collection of Original Receipts which have never appeared in Print, in every Branch of Cookery, Confectionary, &c.

Doncaster, printed for the Authoress by D. Boys, and Sold by Mess. F. & C. Rivington, St. Paul's Church-Yard, London. M DCC XCV.

(Entered at Stationers' Hall)

A third edition was published in 1805. The authoress apologizes for her book as being smaller than others of a similar nature, and perhaps a lower price, but states that the size arises from her attempt 'to avoid that Repetition which is the sole Cause of their Prolixity'. The book is a large octavo of 173 pages. There is a half-title before the title-page.

1797 THE ACCOMPLISHED HOUSEKEEPER, AND UNIVERSAL COOK,

containing all the various Branches of Cookery; Directions for Roasting, Boiling and Made Dishes, also for Frying, Broiling, Stewing, Mincing, and Hashing.

The different Methods of Dressing Poultry, Game, and Fish, and of Preparing Soups, Gravies, Cullices, and Broths,

To dress Roots and Vegetables, and to make all Sorts of Pies, Puddings, Pancakes, and Fritters; Cakes, Puffs, and Biscuits, Cheesecakes, Tarts, and Custards; Creams and Jams; Blanc Mange, Flummery, Jellies, and Syllabubs.

The various Articles in Candying, Drying, Preserves, and Pickling;

The Preparation of Hams, Tongues, Bacon, and of Made Wines and Cordial Waters.

Directions for Carving.

With a Catalogue of the various Articles in Season every Month in the Year.

By T. Williams, and the Principal Cooks at the London and Crown and Anchor Taverns.

London, printed for J. Scatcherd, No. 12, Ave-Maria-Lane. 1797.

[Price Three Shillings Sewed]

This is an abridgement of 'The Universal Cook' by Collingwood and Woollams.

1797 THE LONDON COMPLETE ART OF COOKERY, containing the most approved Receipts ever exhibited to the Public; selected with Care from the newest Editions of the best Authors, French and English.

Also the Complete Brewer; explaining the Art of Brewing Porter, Ale, Twopenny, and Table-Beer; including the proper Management of the Vault or Cellar.

London, printed for William Lane, at the Minerva-Press, Leadenhall-Street. M DCC XCVII.

This is a book of 232 pages which seems copied from Farley's London Art of Cookery, and was probably a fraudulent imitation. The frontispiece represents two men in a kitchen.

1797. THE ACCOMPLISHED FAMILY COOK; being a Complete System of Cookery, adapted to the Tables not only of the Opulent, but of Persons of moderate Fortune and Condition.

By A. Glasse, Twenty Years Cook to several Families of Distinction.

London, printed for J. Bell, No. 148, Oxford Street; Simmonds, Pater Noster Row.

The full title-page is not given as it is merely that of The French Family Cook. The book was probably a failure and the name of Glasse added to stimulate the sale.

1798 AN ECONOMICAL AND NEW METHOD OF COOKERY;

describing upwards of Eighty Cheap, Wholesome, and Nourishing Dishes, consisting of Roast, Boiled, and Baked Meats; Stews, Fries, and above Forty Soups; a Variety of Puddings, Pies, &c. with new and useful Observations on Rice, Barley, Pease, Oatmeal, and Milk, and the numerous Dishes they afford,

Adapted to the Necessity of the Times, equally in all Ranks of Society.

By Eliza Melroe.

" Œconomy is the source of Plenty."
" Bury not your Talent."

London, printed and published for the Author, by C. Chapple, No. 66, Pall-Mall; sold also by T. N. Longman, Paternoster-Row, and all other Booksellers in Town and Country.

Price 2s. 6d. or six for 10s. 6d. if purchased by Clubs of the labouring Poor, or intended for their Use.

1798. Entered at Stationer's Hall.

This is a pamphlet of 94 pages, one of several issued at this time owing to the scarcity of bread. They contain recipes for soups and other cheap foods. Others are:

1795. Useful suggestions favourable to the comfort of the labouring people and of decent housekeepers.

1795 (c.) Hints for the relief of the poor.

1797. An account of a meat and soup charity.

1799. The Economy of an institution, established in Spitalfields, London, for the purpose of supplying the poor with a good meat soup.

1800. Suggestions offered to the consideration of the public.

1800 (c.) THE HOUSEKEEPER'S VALUABLE PRE-
SENT ;
or, Lady's Closet Companion, being a New and Complete
Art of Preparing Confects, according to Modern Practice.
Comprized under the following Parts ; viz.
  I. Different Methods and Degrees of boiling and clarify-
     ing Sugar.
 II. Methods of preserving various Fruits in Syrups, &c.
III. Methods of making Marmalades, Jams, Pastes, &c.
 IV. Methods of making Syrups, Custards, Jellies, Blanch-
     mange, Conserves, Syllabubs, &c.
  V. Methods of preserving various Fruits in Brandy.
 VI. Methods of making a Variety of Biscuits, rich Cakes,
     &c. &c.
VII. Methods of mixing, freezing, and working Ice Creams.
VIII. Methods of preparing Cordials and made Wines.
With a Variety of other useful and elegant Articles.
By Robert Abbot, late Apprentice to Messrs Negri &
Gunter, Confectioners, in Berkeley Square.
Printed for the Author ; and Sold by C. Cooke, No. 17,
Pater-noster Row ; and all other Booksellers in Town and
Country.

   [Price 2s. sewed, or 2s. 6d. neatly bound.]

A little book of 100 pages.

1800 (c.) THE COOK & CONFECTIONER'S GUIDE ;
or Female's Instructor, in Cookery, Confectionary, Making
Wines, Preserving, Pickles, &c.
With every necessary information connected with the above
Arts.
By W. Carter.
London, printed for Bailey and Co. Booksellers.
Price Sixpence.

A paper-covered pamphlet of 32 pages.

ENGLISH COOKERY BOOKS

1800 THE COMPLETE BRITISH COOK ;
being a Collection of the most valuable and useful Receipts, for rendering the whole Art of Cookery plain and familiar to every capacity :
Containing Directions for

Gravies,	Stewing,	Pies,	Pickles,
Sauces,	Hashes,	Tarts,	Syllabubs,
Roasting,	Soups,	Cakes,	Creams,
Boiling,	Fricasees,	Puddings,	Flummeries,
Frying,	Ragouts,	Fritters,	Jellies,
Broiling,	Pastries,	Preserves,	Custards, &c. &c.

By Mary Holland, Professed Cook.
London, printed by J. D. Bewick, Westmoreland Buildings, Aldersgate Street ; for West and Hughes, Paternoster Row ; and sold by all Booksellers. 1800.

A pamphlet of 104 pages. There is a frontispiece representing a kitchen. This is probably the first edition of 'The Complete Economical Cook' of which the sixth edition is entered under 1830, as some of the recipes are identical.

1800 (c.) THE LADIES BEST COMPANION ;
or, A Golden Treasury for the Fair Sex.
Containing the whole Arts of

Cookery,	Potting,	Candying,
Pastry,	Pickling,	Collaring,
Confectionary,	Preserving,	Brewing, &c.

With plain Instructions for making English Wines, from Fruits, Flowers, &c.
To which is added the Art of preserving Beauty, containing the best and easiest Methods of preparing and making Washes, Essences, and Perfumes, &c. for the Hands, Neck, Face, and Hair, in such a Manner as in a great Measure to delay the Ravages of Time on the Features of the Fair Sex.
Likewise Directions for sweetening the Breath, easing the Tooth-ache, preserving the Teeth and Gums, &c. With

many other Articles equally useful to the Fair Sex in General.

> Here Cooks may learn with wond'rous Ease
> The longing Appetite to please ;
> The Art of Beauty how to reach,
> By skilful Methods too we teach ;
> The Fair who with our Rules comply,
> May catch the Heart, and charm the Eye.

By Mrs. Amelia Chambers.

To which are added Every Lady her own and Family's Physician, Consisting of approved physical Receipts for most Disorders that grown People and young Children are Subject to. Also the Family Instructor, containing Directions for cleaning Silks, Lace and Furniture, taking out Spots from Linen and Cloaths, &c. &c. And great Variety of other Articles too numerous to be inserted in a Title Page.

London, printed for J. Cooke, No. 17, in Pater-Noster-Row.
[Price Two Shillings Sewed]

There is the frontispiece of a kitchen which is in Caroline Butler's New London and Country Cook, but with the lines :

> Choice Viands and a skilful Cook invite
> The Puny and Capacious appetite.
> Then let Politeness, Join'd to hunger, haste
> And learn the Method how to Dine in Taste.

A book of 196 pages. The medical part is good and the beauty recipes are fair. They are for such objects as 'To make the Forehead appear extremely Beautiful and engaging', 'To change the Colour of red Eyebrows to a fine Black', &c.

1800 (c.) DOMESTIC MANAGEMENT,

or The Art of Conducting a Family ; with Instructions to Servants in general.

Addressed to Young Housekeepers.

The best of Presents to Servants of all Denominations.

London, printed for H. D. Symonds, at the Literary Press, No. 62, Wardour-Street, Soho.

A book of 108 pages on the duties of servants. If the footman is ordered at dinner to break the claw of a lobster, he is not ' to crack it between the hinges of the dining-room door, but take it into the kitchen'. When sent on a wet day for a hackney-coach, he is not to get into it and ride home. ' This will render it uncomfortably damp.' ' Should a chamber maid be rung for in the night, she should fly to the room, with all speed, as soon as she hears it, and take her tinder-box with her. She may not be aware of the consequences of a moment's delay. Many a life has been lost by the night-mare, for want of momentary assistance ; and a person who has just power to ring the bell, may be suffocated, whilst a maid stays to rub her eyes, light her candle, or adjust her cap. Her tinder-box, of course, ought to be in good order, and near her bed-side.' ' Wages are now large, and it will afford a sufficient change of dress.'

1800 (c.) THE NEW LONDON FAMILY COOK : or, Town and Country Housekeeper's Guide, comprehending Directions for Marketing, with illustrative Plates, on a Principle entirely new ; General Observations, and Bills of Fare for every Week in the Year ; practical Instructions for preparing Soups, Broths, Gravies, Sauces and Made Dishes ; and for dressing Fish, Venison, Hares, Butcher's Meat, Poultry, Game, &c. in all their Varieties.

With the respective Branches of Pastry and Confectionary, the Art of Potting, Pickling, Preserving, &c. Cookery for the Sick, and for the Poor ; Directions for Carving ; and a Glossary of the most generally received French and English Terms in the Culinary Art.

Also a Collection of Valuable Family Recipes, in Dyeing, Perfumery, &c.

Instructions for Brewing, Making of British Wines, Distilling, Managing the Dairy, and Gardening.

And an Appendix, containing general Directions for Servants relative to the Cleaning of Household Furniture, Floor-Cloths, Stoves, Marble, Chimney-Pieces, &c. forming in the whole a most complete Family Instructor.

By Duncan Macdonald, late Head Cook at the Bedford Tavern and Hotel, Covent Garden : and Assistants.

London, printed and published by J. Robins and Co. Ivy Lane, Paternoster Row.

A book of 630 pages which seems to be very complete. There is a portrait of the author as frontispiece.

1800 (c.) THE GUIDE TO PREFERMENT:
or, Powell's Complete Book of Cookery.
Containing the Newest and Best Receipts in Cookery for,

Roasting	Collaring	Cheesecakes
Boiling	Salting and Drying	Custards
Broiling	Soops, Broth, &	Jellies
Frying	Gravy	Conserving
Fricaseys	Bakeing	Candying
Hashing	Pies and Pastes	Preserving and
Stewing	Tartes	Confectionary
Force-Meats	Puddings	Pickling
Potting	Cakes	Makeing Wines
Ragoos		

Likewise the best Methods of Marketing, to know the Goodness or Badness of each particular sort of Eatables, that you want to buy of the Butchers, Poulterers, Fishmongers, Cheesemongers, Pork Shops, Ham Shops, Bacon Wharehouses, Egg Wharehouses, &c. And to prevent being Cheated.

With the forms of placing Dishes on a Table, either in the Middling or Genteelest Taste.

Very Necessary for Ladies, Gentlemen, and their Servants. Price, 1s. 6d.

Bailey Printer, Leadenhall-Street, No. 110.

An octavo of 184 pages, with a frontispiece of a kitchen.

1801 THE ART OF COOKERY MADE EASY AND REFINED;
comprising ample Directions for preparing every Article requisite for furnishing the Tables of the Nobleman, Gentleman, and Tradesman.

ENGLISH COOKERY BOOKS 131

By John Mollard, Cook ; one of the Proprietors of Freemasons' Tavern, Great Queen Street, Lincoln's Inn Fields.

London, printed for the Author, and sold by J. Nunn, Great Queen Street, Lincoln's Inn Fields. 1801.

T. Bensley, Printer, Bolt Court, Fleet Street.

Other editions are 1802 (2), 1807 (3), 1808 (4), 1836 (new).

A large octavo of 314 pages. The preface gives the qualities essential to the completion of a thorough cook—' an acute taste, a fertile invention, and a rigid attention to cleanliness '. There is a half-title.

1802 THE ART OF COOKERY MADE PLAIN AND EASY ;

excelling any Thing of the Kind ever yet published.

Containing

Directions how to Market ; the Season of the Year for Butchers' meat, Poultry, Fish, &c.	Pies.
	Variety of Dishes for Lent, which may be made Use of any other Time.
How to roast and boil to Perfection every Thing necessary to be sent up to Table.	Gravies.
	Sauces.
	Hashes.
	Fricassees,
Vegetables.	Ragouts,
Broiling.	To cure Hams, Bacon, &c.
Frying.	Pickling.
To dress Fish.	Making Cakes.
Made Dishes.	Jellies.
Poultry.	Preserving.
Soups and Broths.	Made Wines. &c. &c. &c.
Puddings.	&c.

Carefully selected from, and containing all the most useful Receipts of Mrs. Glasse.

Ornamented with Engravings, explaining the Method used by the London Butchers in cutting up Meat ; with the Names of the different Joints ; and a Variety of Cuts, shewing the Art of Trussing and Carving.

London, printed by T. Maiden, Sherbourne Lane, for Ann Lemoine, Whiterose-Court, Coleman-Street, and sold by T. Hurst, Paternoster-Row.

[Price One Shilling; or neatly Half-bound, One Shilling and Sixpence.]

A pamphlet of 96 pages. The first engraving is dated 1802.

1802 THE FAMILY FRIEND,

or Housekeeper's Instructor: containing a very complete collection of original & approved receipts in every branch of cookery, confectionary, &c.

By Priscilla Haslehurst, who lived twelve years as housekeeper in the families of Wm. Bethell, Esq. of Rice Park, near Beverley; Mrs. Joddrell, of Manchester; and others of the greatest respectability.

Sheffield; printed by J. Montgomery, Iris-Office, Hartshead. 1802.

An octavo of 156 pages, with a list at the end of over 300 copies subscribed. The authoress was for over twenty years 'a confectioner and instructor of young persons' in Sheffield. A seventh edition, undated, is a large octavo of 215 pages, with a frontispiece to illustrate the art of carving 'engraved for Thompson's edition of Mrs. Haslehurst's Cookery'. There are some curious recipes, e.g. 'To goosify a shoulder of lamb'.

1802 AN ESSAY ON ABSTINENCE FROM ANIMAL FOOD, as a Moral Duty.

By Joseph Ritson.

> Unde fames homini vetitorum tanta ciborum,
> Audetes vesci, genus ô mortale? quod oro,
> Ne facite; et monitis animos advertite nostris.
> OVIDIUS.

London, printed for Richard Phillips, No. 71, St. Pauls Church-Yard. 1802.

Wilks and Taylor, Printers, Chancery-Lane.

No recipes are given.

ENGLISH COOKERY BOOKS

1804 CULINA FAMULATRIX MEDICINÆ:
or, Receipts in Cookery, worthy the notice of those Medical Practitioners, who ride in their Chariots with a Footman behind, and who receive Two-Guinea Fees from their Rich and Luxurious Patients.
By Ignotus.

Propera Stomachum laxare Saginis,
Et tua servatum consume in Saecula Rhombum.
JUV.

York, printed by T. Wilson and R. Spence, High-Ousegate: and sold by J. Mawman, Bookseller in the Poultry, London. 1804.

Other editions are 1805 (2), 1806 (4), 1807 (5), 1810 (new). The author was A. Hunter, M.D., F.R.S., who practised at York.

The frontispiece is a huge pig with the word 'Transmigration'. The book is dedicated 'To those Gentlemen who freely give two guineas for a Turtle Dinner at the Tavern, when they might have a more wholesome one at Home for ten shillings'.

1804 THE HOUSEKEEPER'S INSTRUCTOR;
or Universal Family Cook, being a full and clear Display of the Art of Cookery in all its Branches. Containing

Proper Directions for dressing all Kinds of Butcher's Meat, Poultry, Game, Fish, &c.

The Method of preparing all the Varieties of Soups, Hashes, and Made Dishes.

The whole Art of Confectionary, Pickling, Preserving, &c.

The making and keeping in Perfection British Wines; and

Proper Rules for Brewing Malt Liquor for large or small Families.

To which is added the Complete Art of Carving, illustrated with Engravings, explaining by proper References, the Manner in which Young Practitioners may acquit themselves at Table with Elegance and Ease. Also,

Bills of Fare for every Month in the Year.

The Manner of decorating a Table, displayed by Copper Plates.

Directions for Marketing,

Observations on Culinary Poisons, and

The Management of the Kitchen and Fruit Garden.

By W. A. Henderson, many Years eminent in the Culinary Profession.
The Twelfth Edition.
Corrected, revised, and considerably improved, by every modern Additional Variation in the Art,
By Jacob Christopher Schnebbelie, late apprentice to Messrs. Tupp and Perry, Oxford-Street; afterwards principal cook at Melun's Hotel, Bath; and now of the Albany, London.
London: printed and Sold by J. Stratford, No. 112, Holborn-Hill. 1804.

There is a portrait of Schnebbelie with a view of the south side of the Albany as preface. The previous editions are by Henderson alone, and undated. Most, if not all, have a kitchen as frontispiece, with a quaint 'explanation'. Other editions are 1805 (also 12), 1807 (14), 1809 (15), 1811 (17). The eleventh, seventeenth, and twentieth editions are undated.

1804 THE NEW PRACTICE of Cookery, Pastry, Baking, and Preserving: being The Country Housewife's Best Friend.
By Mrs. Hudson & Mrs. Donat, present and late housekeepers and cooks to Mrs. Buchan Hepburn of Smeaton, and Published by Her Permission.
Edinburgh: printed by J. Moir, Royal Bank Close, and sold by the editors. 1804.

A small book of 242 pages. Watt gives 1798 as the date, but there is no indication that the 1804 edition is not the first. The editors 'offer to the world, not a cobweb theory of cookery, such as the flimsy constitution-mongers of France have spun for these 12 or 15 years past out of their distempered brains, to deceive and ruin that miserable people: No! here facts only are narrated'.

1806 A COMPLETE SYSTEM OF COOKERY,
on a plan entirely new, consisting of every thing that is requisite for cooks to know in the kitchen business; containing Bills of Fare for every day in the year, and

directions to dress each dish ; being one year's work, at the Marquis of Buckingham's,

From the 1st of January, to the 31st of December, 1805.

By John Simpson, present cook to the most noble the Marquis of Buckingham.

London, printed for W. Stewart, opposite Albany, Piccadilly. 1806.

Other editions are 1807 (2), 1813 (3), 1822 (4). There is an undated edition of 1807 and one of 1816, which claims to be revised and rewritten by Simpson. In 1834 appeared 'Simpson's Cookery Improved and Modernised', by Henderson William Brand, of the kitchen of his late Majesty George IV, which is practically a different book. The original book is on an entirely new plan. There are 366 bills of fare, and following each is the method of cooking the several dishes. There is a half-title. Our forefathers must have risen early, as the preface advises that 'in the summer time, cooks should be very exact with the butchers ; and make them bring their meat in not later than six o'clock in the morning'.

1807 THE FAMILY DIRECTOR ;

or, Housekeeper's Assistant : containing upwards of Three Hundred Original Receipts, in Pastry, Pickling, Preserving, Collaring, Making Wines, &c,

By Addison Ashburn.

Coventry, printed for the Author by N. Merridew. Sold by Longman, Hurst, Rees, and Orme, London ; the Author, at Meriden ; N. Merridew, Coventry ; Belcher and Son, Birmingham ; and W. Perry, Warwick. 1807.

A book of 180 pages, with a modest preface.

1807 A NEW SYSTEM OF DOMESTIC COOKERY ;

formed upon Principles of Economy, and adapted to the Use of Private Families.

By a Lady.

A new edition, corrected.

London, printed for John Murray, Fleet-Street ; J. Harding, St. James's-Street ; and A. Constable and Co. Edinburgh ;

at the Union Printing-Office, St. John's Square, by W. Wilson. 1807.

Price Seven Shillings and Sixpence.

This book, by Mrs. Maria Eliza Rundle (1745–1828), rivalled Mrs. Glasse in popularity. It is a duodecimo of 351 pages, with a frontispiece representing a larder. According to the D. N. B. the first edition was published in 1808. The sixty-fourth edition was published in 1840, and the sixty-fifth in 1841, and in an amended form the book appeared as late as 1893.

In the British Museum is 'Mrs. Rundle's Young Housekeeper's Pocket Account Book', which was issued with an interleaved almanac in 1843, and perhaps in other years. There are a few recipes in it.

1808 THE LINCOLNSHIRE FAMILY JEWEL;
or, The Art of Cookery made Plain and Easy.
Lincoln, printed and sold by John Drury, near the Stone-Row. 1808.

A chap-book of 34 pages.

1808 THE TOWN AND COUNTRY COOKERY,
or Housekeeper's Companion; containing a Number of the most useful and economical Receipts in Cookery.
London, printed and sold by R. Harrild, 20, Great Eastcheap. 1808.

A chap-book of 36 pages with a rude coloured frontispiece.

1809 THE IMPERIAL AND ROYAL COOK:
consisting of the most sumptuous made Dishes, Ragouts, Fricassees, Soups, Gravies, &c. Foreign and English: including the latest Improvements in Fashionable Life.
By Frederic Nutt, Esq. Author of the Complete Confectioner, &c.
London, printed for Matthews and Leigh, Strand, by James Moyes, Shoe Lane. 1809.

This is a book designed for 'opulent families . . . who wish to give handsome occasional entertainments to their select friends'.

1809 THE COMPLETE CONFECTIONER AND FAMILY COOK ;

including all the late improvements in

Confectionary,	Jellies,	Baking,
Preserving,	Creams,	Cookery,
Pickling,	Pastry,	&c. &c.

With many valuable Receipts and ample Directions for Marketing, Trussing, Carving, &c.

The whole being the result of many Years Practice and Experience.

By J. Caird.

Illustrated with Copperplates and Wooden Cuts.

Leith, printed by and for Archibald Allardice and the Author, Old Assembly Close, Edinburgh. 1809.

A book of 454 pages with a frontispiece of a confectioner in his kitchen. The main part is devoted to confectionery.

1810 THE NEW FAMILY RECEIPT-BOOK,

containing seven hundred truly valuable Receipts in various Branches of Domestic Economy ; selected from the Works of British and Foreign Writers of unquestionable Experience & Authority, and from the attested Communications of Scientific Friends.

> " What lookest thou ?
> Good Lessons for thee, and thy wife ?
> Then keep them in memory fast,
> To help as a comfort to Life."   TUSSER.

London, printed by Squire and Warwick, Furnival's-Inn-Court, for John Murray, 32, Fleet-Street, sold also by every Bookseller and Newsman in Town and Country. 1810.

Price Seven Shillings and Sixpence.

[Entered at Stationers' Hall]

By Mrs. Rundle, a supplement to ' A New System of Domestic Cookery '. Editions in 1811 and 1815 contain eight hundred recipes.

1810 THE HOUSEKEEPER'S DOMESTIC LIBRARY;
or, New universal family Instructor in Practical Economy. Containing the whole Art of Cookery, in all its New and Fashionable Varieties; with proper Instructions for Baking, Roasting, Boiling, Broiling, Frying, Hashing, Stewing, Fricaseeing, Ragooing, with Confectionary in all its Branches:

Potting and Collaring Fish and Meat.	Brewing of Porter, Ale, Beer, and Table-Beer.
Salting and Curing Hams, Tongues, Bacon, Beef, Pork, &c.	Distilling of Spirits, Simple Waters, Compounds, and Cordials.
Pickling of every Description.	Making and Keeping Choice Wines.

Also, the complete Art of Carving, and Performing the Honours of the Table with Grace and Propriety.

Likewise new Bills of Fare: Made Dishes of all Descriptions; Directions for Marketing; &c. &c.

By Charles Millington.

London, printed by W. Flint, Old Bailey, for M. Jones, No. 5, Newgate Street; C. Chapple, Pall Mall; and J. Booth, Duke Street, Portland Chapel. 1810.

A large octavo of 403 pages. There is a frontispiece representing a turtle and a deer; several plates follow the title-page.

1810 THE FEMALE ECONOMIST;
or A Plain System of Cookery, for the Use of Families, containing upwards of Eight Hundred and Fifty Valuable Receipts. By Mrs. Smith.

" In every station, an Economist is a respectable character."
HUNTER'S CULINÆ.

Fifth Edition.

London, printed for Samuel Leigh, 18, Strand. 1817.
Four Shillings Boards.

Watt gives the date as 1810. There is an edition of 1823. There is a frontispiece representing game on a table. The Family Medicine is short but good and free from nastiness.

ENGLISH COOKERY BOOKS

1810 DOMESTIC MANAGEMENT ;
or, The Healthful Cookery-Book.
To which is prefixed a Treatise on Diet, as the surest Means to preserve Health, Long Life, &c.
With many valuable Observations on the nutritious and beneficial, as well as the injurious Effects of various Kinds of Food ;
Also Remarks on the wholesome and pernicious Modes of Cookery, intended as an Antidote to modern Errors therein.
To which is added the Method of treating such trifling Medical Cases as properly come within the Sphere of Domestic Management.
By a Lady.
London, printed for B. Crosby and Co. Stationers'-Court, Paternoster Row and sold by every Bookseller in the United Kingdom.
Price 5s. boards. 1810
J. G. Barnard, Printer, Skinner-street, London.

<small>A duodecimo of 355 pages, doubtless produced to rival Mrs. Rundle's New System of Domestic Cookery. Its object, according to the preface, ' is to temper instead of to pamper the appetite '. Watt gives Domestic Management of 1810 as being by Arabella Plumptre.</small>

1810 (c.) THE BRITISH HOUSEWIFE ;
containing the most approved Receipts in Roasting, Boiling, Frying, Broiling and Stewing ; also The Complete Brewer ; explaining the Art of brewing Porter, Ale ; Twopenny, and Table Beer ; including the particular Directions for making British Wines.
London, printed for William Lane, Leadenhall-Street.

<small>A pamphlet of 72 pages. There is a frontispiece of men entering a dining-room.</small>

1811 THE YOUNG WOMAN'S COMPANION :
or, Frugal Housewife. Containing the most approved Methods of Pickling, Preserving, Potting, Collaring, Confectionary, Managing and Colouring Foreign Wines and Spirits, making English Wines, Compounds, &c. &c.

Also the Art of Cookery, containing Directions for dressing all kinds Butchers Meat, Poultry, Game, Fish, &c. &c. &c.

With the Complete Art of Carving, illustrated and made plain by Engravings.

Likewise Instructions for Marketing. With the Theory of brewing Malt Liquor.

To which are added, Directions for Letter Writing, Drawing, Painting, &c. and several valuable miscellaneous pieces.

Manchester, printed by Russell and Allen, Deansgate. 1811.

A large octavo of 540 pages. There was another edition in 1813. The book is full of words of wisdom. ' But, on the other hand, there is a kind of neatness, which gives a lady the air of a housemaid, and makes her excessively troublesome to every body, and particularly to her husband.' ' A white hand is a very desirable ornament ; and a hand can never be white unless it be kept clean. Nor is this all ; for if the young lady will excel her companions in this respect, she must keep her hands in constant motion, which will occasion the blood to circulate freely, and have a wonderful effect. The motion I would recommend, is working at her needle, brushing up the house, or twirling the distaff. It was this industry in our grandmothers which gave Kneller an opportunity of gratifying posterity with the view of so many fine hands and arms in his incomparable portraits.'

1811 THE RETURN TO NATURE,
or, A Defence of the Vegetable Regimen ; with some Account of an Experiment made during the last three or four years in the Author's Family.

> Man, only man, Creation's Lord confess'd,
> Amidst his happy realm remains unbless'd ;
> On the bright earth, his flow'r-embroider'd throne,
> Th' imperial mourner reigns and weeps alone.
>   SPENCER'S YEAR OF SORROW.

By John Frank Newton, Esq.
Part the first.
London, printed for T. Cadell and W. Davies, Strand, by
J. McCreery, Black-Horse-Court. 1811.

No recipes are given. Some of the statements in the book are strange. 'Considering what are the disgusting offices which ill health entails upon servants, the attendants of the sick, it seems a merciful dispensation in their behalf that the sense of smelling should be universally deficient in them.'

1811 THE ART OF PRESERVING all kinds of animal and vegetable substances for several years.
A work published by order of the French minister of the interior, on the report of the Board of Arts and Manufactures.
By M. Appert.
Translated from the French.
London, printed for Black, Parry, and Kingsbury, booksellers to the Hon. East-India Company, Leadenhall Street. 1811.

There is a frontispiece of machinery used in corking bottles. There is a half-title. The original appeared in 1810.

1812 THE FRUGAL HOUSEKEEPER'S COMPANION:
being a complete System of Cookery, the result of thirty-six years' actual experience, in some of the most respectable Families in the Kingdom: containing a great number of original recipes in modern cooking, pickling, preserving, &c; The art of confectionary, and of making jellies, jams, creams, &c; Bills of Fare for every month in the year; Directions for marketing; The art of carving, &c.
By Elizabeth Alcock.
Liverpool, printed by James Smith, sold by the Author, No. 71, Byrom-Street; and by Isaac Clarke and Co., Manchester. 1812.

An octavo of 263 pages. There are a few medical recipes at the end. The author states that the cure for rheumatism, made of garlic, cloves, and gum ammonia, and taken with strong saxafrage tea, ' is a very famous receipt, one hundred pounds has been given for it '.

1813 THE FRENCH COOK;

or, The Art of Cookery developed in all its various Branches. By Louis Eustache Ude, formerly cook to Louis XVI. King of France, and at present cook to the Right Hon. Earl of Sefton.

London, printed by Cox and Baylis, Great Queen Street, Lincoln's-Inn-Fields, for the Author, and sold by J. Ebers, 27, Old Bond Street; and may be had of all the Booksellers in the United Kingdom. 1813.

There is a portrait of the author as frontispiece. Other editions are 1814 (2), 1822 (7), 1827 (8), 1829 (10), 1835 (13). There is a half-title.

1814 THE SCHOOL FOR GOOD LIVING;

or, a literary and historical essay on the European kitchen: beginning with Cadmus the cook and king, and concluding with the Union of Cookery and Chymistry.

> Ἀρχη και ρίζα παντος αγαθοῦ, ἡ της
> Γαστρὸς ἡδονη.—Athen. Deip. l. 7. c. 5.
>
> Sequitur sua quemque Culina.   Juv.

London, printed by J. Gillet, Crown-court, Fleet-street, for H. Colburn, Conduit-Street; sold also by G. Goldie, Edinburgh; and J. Cumming, Dublin. 1814.

This is not a cookery book, but is interesting since it gives lists of writers on cookery. There was a second edition in 1822 with the title ' Gastronomy, or, the School for Good Living '. The author writes from Bath. I have not been able to find all the English writers he names.

1815 THE EPICURE'S ALMANACK;

or, Calendar of Good Living: containing a Directory to the Taverns, Coffee-houses, Inns, Eating-houses, and other Places of alimentary Resort in the British Metropolis and

its Environs : a Review of Artists who administer to the Wants and Enjoyments of the Table ; a Survey of the Markets ; and a Calendar of the Meats in Season during each Month of the Year.
To be continued Annually.

> —navibus atque
> Quadrigis petimus bene vivere ; quod petis hîc est
> HOR.

London, printed for Longman, Hurst, Rees, Orme, and Brown, Paternoster-Row. 1815.

A duodecimo of 351 pages on the model of the 'Almanach des Gourmands'.

1815 THE FEMALE INSTRUCTOR ;

or, Young Woman's Companion : being a Guide to all the Accomplishments which adorn the Female Character, either as a useful Member of Society, a pleasing and instructive Companion, or, a respectable Mother of a Family.
With many pleasing Examples of illustrious Females.
To which are added useful Medicinal Receipts, and a concise system of Cookery, with other valuable Information in the different Branches of Domestic Economy.
" Favour is deceitful, and Beauty is vain ; but a Woman that feareth the Lord, she shall be praised." SOLOMON.
Liverpool, printed by Nuttall, Fisher, and Dixon, Duke Street.
Stereotype Edition.

The frontispiece, representing two young women sewing and reading, is dated 1815. There was a reprint in 1816 with a different frontispiece. The book is a large octavo of 560 pages on the lines of The Young Woman's Companion of 1811.

1817 MODERN DOMESTIC COOKERY,

and useful Receipt Book ; containing the most approved Directions for Purchasing, Preserving, and Cooking Meat, Fish, Poultry, Game, &c. in all their Varieties ; Trussing and Carving ; Preparing Soups, Gravies, Sauces, Made

Dishes, Potting, Pickling, &c. with all the Branches of Pastry and Confectionary, a complete Family Physician, Instructions to Servants for the best Methods of performing their various Duties, Art of Making British Wines, Brewing, Baking, &c.
By Elizabeth Hammond.
London, printed and sold by Dean and Munday, Threadneedle-Street. 1817.

The seventh edition, undated, has a frontispiece and an engraved title-page. The ninth edition is also undated. The 1817 edition is a duodecimo of 288 pages. The Family Physician recommends 'cataplasms of fresh cow-dung' for bruises. 'Iliac passion' seems to be the name for appendicitis, 'a dangerous disorder which in many instances will not be controuled by medicine.'

1817 (*c.*) THE FAMILY RECEIPT-BOOK;
or, Universal Repository of Useful Knowledge and Experience in all the various Branches of Domestic Œconomy, including Scarce, Curious, and Valuable, Select Receipts, and Choice Secrets, in

Cookery,	Distilling,	Gilding,	Gardening,
Medicine,	Pickling,	Painting,	Hunting,
Confectionary,	Preserving,	Varnishing,	Fishing,
Pastry,	Perfumery,	Agriculture,	Fowling,
Brewing,	Dyeing,	Farriery,	&c. &c. &c.

With Specifications of Approved Patent Medicines; all the most serviceable Preparations for Domestic Purposes; and numerous successful Improvements in the Ornamental as well as Useful Arts, Manufactures, &c.
Extracted from the Records of the Patent Office; and translated from foreign Books and Journals, in all the Languages of Europe.
The whole forming a compleat Library of Valuable Domestic Knowledge, and General Œconomy; selected from the Experience of Ages, and combined with all the chief Modern Discoveries and Improvements of our own and other Countries, in those Useful and Elegant Arts which

not only contribute to the Happiness, the Convenience, and the Comfort, of Civilized and Social Life, but even to the Preservation and Prolongation of Life itself.

London, printed for the Editors, and published by Oddy and Co. 27, Oxford Street ; and C. La Grange, London.

[Third Edition, price 25s. boards.]

A large quarto of 584 pages.

1817 THE NEW FAMILY RECEIPT-BOOK.
By D. Hughson, L.L.D.

London, printed for W. Pritchard, 36, Warwick-Lane, Newgate Street ; and J. Bysh, 52, Paternoster Row. 1817.

A large quarto of 384 pages with a title-page almost exactly corresponding to that of The Family Receipt-Book. Many of the recipes are similar, and this book seems to be an abbreviated edition of the other.

1817 APICIUS REDEVIVUS ; OR, THE COOK'S ORACLE :

wherein especially the Art of composing Soups, Sauces, and Flavouring Essences is made so clear and easy, by the Quantity of each Article being accurately stated by Weight and Measure, that every one may soon learn to dress a Dinner, as well as the most experienced Cook ;

Being Six Hundred Receipts, the Result of Actual Experiments instituted in the Kitchen of a Physician, for the Purpose of composing a Culinary Code for the Rational Epicure, and augmenting the Alimentary Enjoyments of Private Families ;

Combining Economy with Elegance ; and saving Expense to Housekeepers, and Trouble to Servants.

" I have taken as much pains in describing, in the fullest manner, how to make, in the easiest, most agreeable, and most economical way, those Dishes which daily contribute to the comforts of the middle rank of Society, as I have in directing the preparation of those piquante and elaborate relishes, the most ingenious and accomplished 'Officers of the Mouth' have invented for the amusement of Grands Gourmands. These are so composed, as to be as agreeable and useful to the stomach, as they are inviting to the appetite ; nourishing without being inflammatory, and savoury without being surfeiting."—Vide Preface, page 3. London, printed for Samuel Bagster, No. 15, Paternoster-Row, by J. Moyes, Greville Street. 1817.

Other editions are 1818 (2), 1821 (3), 1822 (4), 1823 (5), 1823 (6), 1823 (7), 1827, 1831, 1838, 1840. The author was William Kitchiner, M.D., a wealthy physician of London who did not practise his profession. He died in 1827. The first part of the title was dropped in all editions after the first. One of the maxims in the preface is—'Masticate, denticate, chump, grind, and swallow.'

A 'Shilling Kitchiner' was published in 1861.

Other books by the same author are 'Peptic Precepts', 1821 ; 'The Art of Invigorating and Prolonging Life', 1822 ; 'The Housekeeper's Ledger', 1825.

1818 THE FAMILY RECEIPT BOOK ;

containing a great Variety of useful Family Receipts in Housekeeping, Making Wines, &c.

By Mrs. Westcott, late housekeeper to the Right Hon. The Earl of Morley.

Plymouth, printed for the Author, by Haviland and Creagh, (Successors to Haydon and Cobley). 1818.

There is a list of subscribers at the beginning which shows that nearly 250 copies were taken before publication. It is a book of 177 pages. Some of the medical recipes are excellent, and others have very pleasant names, 'Oil of Charity,' 'Live-long; an excellent Stomachic.' But snails are still ordered for the 'Restorative Jelly'.

1819 THE BANQUET in three cantos

οὔτε γαρ θεοὶ
σεμνᾶν χαρίταν ἄτερ
κοιρανέοντι χοροὺς
οὔτε δαῖτας.

PINDAR OLYMP.

London; published by Baldwin, Cradock, and Joy, 47, Paternoster-Row. 1819.

By Hans Busk. There is an engraved title-page, and a frontispiece representing the death of Vatel. The author published in the same year 'The Dessert, a Poem, to which is added The Tea', each part having a frontispiece, the first of grapes, the second of tea.

There was a second edition of both the Banquet and the Dessert in 1820.

1820 THE HOUSEKEEPER'S ACCOMPT-BOOK,

(Improved by Red Lines across the Pages) for the Year 1820; being an easy, concise, and complete method of keeping an exact account of every article made use of in a family throughout the year;

On fifty-two pages, each page containing the sundry articles of housekeeping, and seven columns for the expenses of every day in the week;

With room for occasional memorandums at the bottom.

Also, the following Useful Particulars:

I. Tables of the Window, House, Servants, Horse, Carriage, Taxed-Cart, Dog, Hair-Powder, and Armorial Bearing Dishes, &c.

II. A Table of the Assize and Price of Standard Wheaten Bread, giving the Weight and Price of Bread according to the Price of Wheat, from 5s. to 14s. 6d. the Winchester Bushel.

III. Marketing Tables, giving the price of any number of Pounds, yards, &c. from one Farthing to one Shilling, by the pound, &c.

IV. Tables of Weights, Measures, &c.

V. Table of Expenses, Income, or Wages, by the year, month, week, and day, from $1l$ to 40,000l.

VI. A Catalogue of useful Things necessary to be known by all Persons.

VII. Tables of English and Irish Money equalized.

VIII. Table of the Expenses of every Week in the Year, and of the whole Year, at one view.

IX. The Repository; containing a Variety of useful Receipts in Cookery, &c. &c.

A correct list of Stamps on Bills, Bonds, Receipts, Legacies, &c. &c.

Bath, printed for (and by) R. Cruttwell; and Longman, Hurst, Rees, Orme, and Brown, Pater-noster-Row, London; and Sold by them, and by J. Harris, Corner of St. Paul's Church-Yard; Whitrow, Jewry-Street, Aldgate, London; Beilby and Knott, Birmingham; Constable and Co, Edinburgh; J. Smith and Son, Glasgow; and by all other Booksellers and Stationers in England and Scotland.

To be continued annually. [Price 2s.]

A large quarto which was published for over thirty years. There are recipes at the end of each volume.

1820 COOKERY

By Mrs. Nourse. Fourth edition. Edinburgh. 1820.

The only copy I have seen has lost its title-page. The 'advertisement' to the fourth edition gives the date. The head-line is 'Nourse's Cookery'. It is a small octavo of 336 pages, and seems a good book. 'Chopin' is used for quart and 'mutchkin' for pint. Blackwoods published an edition in 1838, but can trace no earlier edition as published by them.

1820 TABELLA CIBARIA.

The Bill of Fare: a Latin poem, implicitly translated and fully explained in copious and interesting Notes, relating to the Pleasures of Gastronomy, and the mysterious Art of Cookery.

Ipsa memor praecepta canam; celabitur auctor.—HOR.

London, published by Sherwood, Neely, and Jones, Paternoster Row; J. Robins and Co. Ivy Lane, Paternoster Row; and sold by all booksellers. 1820.

A poem 'written several years ago in an idle hour and at the solicitation of a few friends mostly foreigners, who challenged the author upon the apparent impossibility of expressing, in decent Latin verses, the curious and pleasingly tangible variety of dishes which French eating-houses and hotels lavishly display upon their long and hardly intelligible Bills of Fare'. The notes are very interesting. The author was the Abbé Ange-Denis Macquin.

1820 THE MODERN COOKERY,

written upon the most approved and economical principles, and in which every Receipt has stood the Test of Experience.
By a Lady.
Second edition, with considerable editions by the author.
Derby, printed by and for Henry Mozley. 1820.

<small>A duodecimo of 209 pages with a frontispiece representing a larder. There was an eleventh edition in 1868.</small>

1820 THE ITALIAN CONFECTIONER;

or, Complete Economy of Desserts: containing the Elements of the Art, according to the most modern and approved practice.
By G. A. Jarrin, Confectioner, New Bond Street.
Third edition, corrected and enlarged.
London; William H. Ainsworth, Old Bond Street. 1827.

<small>The first edition was 1820 and the second 1823. Other editions were 1831, 1834, 1836, 1841, 1843, 1861. There is a portrait of the author as frontispiece.</small>

1821 PRACTICAL ECONOMY;

or, the application of modern discoveries to the purposes of domestic life.
London: Henry Colburn & Co. Conduit Street, Hanover Square. 1821.

<small>There are a few recipes.</small>

1821 THE MODERN RECEIPT BOOK,

being a collection of nearly eight hundred valuable receipts, arranged under their respective heads; viz. Domestic Economy, Bleaching and Scouring, Dyeing, Tanning, Cements, Varnishes, Lackers, Rural Economy, Management of Bees, Gardening, Brewing, Distilling, Perfumery, Making Wines, the Metallic Arts (including Gilding, Silvering, and Plating,), Drawing and Painting, &c. &c.
The Whole carefully selected from the latest and best

Authorities, and enriched by many original and valuable Communications, confirmed by actual Experiment or personal Observation.

By James Cochrane.

London, printed for A. K. Newman and Co., Leadenhall-Street, and Dean and Munday, Threadneedle-Street. 1821.

There is very little cookery in this book, which was published as a Supplement to Hammond's Modern Domestic Cookery.

1821 A NEW SYSTEM OF VEGETABLE COOKERY: with an Introduction recommending abstinence from animal food and intoxicating liquors.

The second edition.

By a member of the society of Bible-Christians.

Better is a dinner of herbs where love is, than a stalled ox, and hatred therewith. Prov. xv. 17.

It is good neither to eat flesh, nor to drink (intoxicating) wine. Rom. xiv. 21.

Printed at the Academy Press, King-Street, Salford. 1821.
Price Three Shillings and Sixpence in Boards.

A duodecimo of 372 pages. The author has an extraordinary theory that the word fish when met with in the Gospel history should be taken to mean water-melon or lotus-plant. He considers that abstinence from animal food would abolish war, 'for those who are so conscientious as not to kill animals, will never murder human beings.' The medical recipes are poor. 'A roasted onion applied to the top of the head will frequently relieve the most violent pain.' 'A small bag of saffron worn at the stomach prevents sea-sickness.' For dysentery, 'Take a sheet of writing-paper, cut it in slips, boil it in a pint and a half of milk to a pint; take it at twice.'

1821 CULINARY CHEMISTRY,

exhibiting the scientific principles of cookery, with concise instructions for preparing good and wholesome Pickles, Vinegar, Conserves, Fruit Jellies, Marmalades, and various other Alimentary Substances employed in Domestic Economy, with observations on the chemical constitution and nutritive qualities of different kinds of food.

With copper plates.

By Frederick Accum, operative chemist, lecturer on practical chemistry, on mineralogy, and on chemistry applied to the arts and manufactures ; member of the Royal Irish Academy ; fellow of the Linnæan Society ; member of the Royal Academy of Sciences, and of the Royal Society of Arts, Berlin, &c. &c.

London, published by R. Ackermann, 101, Strand, 1821.

<small>There is a coloured frontispiece. The author wrote two other books connected with cookery ; 'A Treatise on Adulterations of Food', 1820, and 'A Treatise on the Art of making Good and Wholesome Bread', 1821.</small>

1822 ESSAYS, MORAL, PHILOSOPHICAL, AND STOMACHICAL,

on the important Science of Good-Living.

Dedicated to the Right Worshipful the Court of Aldermen. By Launcelot Sturgeon, Esq. Fellow of the Beef-Steak Club, and an Honorary Member of several Foreign Pic Nics, &c. &c. &c.

" Eat ! drink ! and be merry !—for to-morrow you die."

London, printed for G. and W. B. Whittaker, 13, Ave-Maria Lane. 1822.

<small>There is a frontispiece representing 'Meditations of an Epicure' The second edition was 1823. Sturgeon is, of course, a pseudonym.</small>

1822 (c.) THE FAMILY CYCLOPÆDIA ;

a Manual of useful and necessary knowledge in Domestic Economy, Agriculture, Chemistry, and the Arts ; including the most approved modes of treatment of diseases, accidents, and casualties.

By James Jennings.

London, printed for Sherwood, Gilbert, and Piper, Paternoster-Row.

<small>A thick volume of 1374 pages with a frontispiece representing a family group. There is not much cookery in it.</small>

1823 FIVE THOUSAND RECEIPTS

in all the Useful and Domestic Arts, constituting a Complete and Universal Practical Library, and Operative Cyclopædia.

Mr. Hobbes, of Malmesbury, thought the accumulation of details a hindrance of learning ; and used to wish that all the Books in the world were embarked in one ship, and that he might be permitted to bore a hole in its bottom. He was right in one sense ; for the Disquisitions and Treatises with which our Libraries are filled, are often merely the husks and shells of knowledge ; but it would be to be wished, that before he were permitted to bore his hole, some literary analysts should select all the Facts, Recipes, and Prescriptions, useful to Man, and condense them into a portable Volume. LOCKE.

By Colin Mackenzie, author of One thousand experiments in manufactures and chemistry.

London, printed for Sir Richard Phillips and Co. and to be had of all booksellers. 1823.

Price 10s. 6d. Bound, or 12s. Calf Gilt.

The third edition was 1824. The book was reprinted in America as late as 1870.

1823 THE COOK AND HOUSEKEEPER'S COMPLETE AND UNIVERSAL DICTIONARY ;

including A System of Modern Cookery, in all its various Branches, adapted to the use of Private Families :

Also a Variety of original and valuable Information, relative to

Baking,	Economy of Poultry,
Brewing,	Family medicine,
Carving,	Gardening,
Cleaning,	Home-made Wines,
Collaring,	Pickling,
Curing,	Potting,
Economy of Bees,	Preserving,
———— of a Dairy,	Rules of Health

and every other Subject connected with Domestic Economy.
By Mrs. Mary Eaton.
Embellished with Engravings.
Bungay, printed and published by J. and R. Childs. 1823.

There is a portrait of the author as frontispiece, also an engraved title-page dated 1822 and a half-title. A new edition was published in 1849. The preface claims that the book is practical and different from most others, concerning which ' a young female, just returned from the hymeneal altar, is ready to exclaim on the first perusal, as the philosopher did who visited the metropolis, How many things are here which I do not want '. The preface is full of interest. ' It is in general a good maxim, to select servants not younger than thirty.' ' The master or mistress who wishes to enjoy the rare luxury of a table well served in the best stile, should treat the cook as a friend ; should watch over her health with peculiar care, and be sure that her taste does not suffer, by her stomach being deranged by bilious attacks. A small proportion of that attention usually bestowed on a favourite horse, or even a dog, would suffice to regulate her animal system.'

1823 THE FOOTMAN'S DIRECTORY,
and Butler's Remembrancer ; or, the Advice of Onesimus to his young Friends : comprising Hints on the Arrangement and Performance of their Work ; Rules for setting out Tables and Sideboards ; the Art of waiting at Table, and conducting large and small Parties ; Directions for cleaning Plate, Glass, Furniture, Clothes, and all other Things which come within the Care of a Man-Servant ; and Advice respecting Behaviour to Superiors, Tradespeople, and Fellow-Servants.
With an Appendix, comprising various useful Receipts and Tables.
London, printed for the Author ; and sold by J. Hatchard and Son, 187, Piccadilly, 1823.

There is a half-title. The author's name, Thomas Cosnett, is given in an edition of 1825, which the preface says is the fifth. The book must have met with much success to have reached a fifth edition so quickly. There are a few cookery recipes in it.

1824 ECONOMICAL COOKERY,

for Young Housekeepers; or, The art of providing good and palatable dishes for a family, without extravagance, being chiefly the result of experience and long practice.

To which are added, Directions for Pickling, Preserving, &c. And a Variety of useful Domestic Recipes.

By a lady.

London, printed for Harvey and Darton, Gracechurch-Street. 1824.

A pamphlet of 129 pages.

1824 COOKERY AND CONFECTIONARY

by John Conrade Cooke

London, printed by B. Bensley, Bolt Court, for W. Simpkin and R. Marshall.

There is also an engraved title, which seems to have been drawn and engraved by the author. The book is a small octavo of 213 pages. At the end are several plates of pastry cutters, wax baskets, &c., drawn by the author. The 'novel feature' of the book, according to the preface, is the having 'set down the requisite time for the cooking of each dish'.

1824 COOKERY MADE EASY:

being a Complete System of Domestic Management, uniting Elegance with Economy.

To which are added, Instructions for trussing and carving, with several descriptive plates; Method of curing and drying Hams and Tongues; Mushroom and Walnut Ketchups, Quin's Sauce, Vinegars, &c. &c.

With other necessary Information for small families, housekeepers, &c.

The whole being the result of actual experience.

By Michael Willis, many years Cook at the Thatched-House Tavern.

London, printed by W. Lewis, 21, Finch-Lane ; for John Bumpus, Holborn Bars ; and may be had of all booksellers. 1824.

A duodecimo of 216 pages. The frontispiece represents two shops—Allbone, Butcher and Wing, Poulterer. An undated edition was published by Orlando Hodgson, Cloth Fair.

1824 THE ECONOMIST,
or, New Family Cookery,
By Anthony Haselmore, many Years Cook in a Nobleman's Family.
London, printed for T. and J. Allman, Princes St. Hanover Square. 1824.

The frontispiece represents a kitchen. There is a supplement of miscellaneous information. The book, without the supplement, was reprinted as Clements' edition of the New Family Cookery.

1824 THE FAMILY ORACLE OF HEALTH ; ECONOMY, MEDICINE, AND GOOD LIVING ;
adapted to all ranks of society, from the palace to the cottage.
By A. F. Crell, MD, FRS, and W. M. Wallace, Esq, assisted by a Committee of Scientific Gentlemen.
London, printed by C. Smith, 163, Strand, Published by J. Walker, 44, Paternoster Row.

This came out in monthly parts from 1824 to 1828. It is more medical than gastronomic.

1824 THE ART OF FRENCH COOKERY.
By A. B. Beauvilliers, Restaurateur, Paris.
London, printed for Longman, Hurst, Rees, Orme, Brown, and Green, Paternoster-Row. 1824.

A duodecimo of 380 pages. There was a third edition in 1827. The French original was published in 1814.

1824-1826 THE ECONOMIST AND GENERAL ADVISER,

containing important papers on the following subjects ;

The markets.	Agriculture.
Marketing.	Public abuses.
Drunkenness.	Shops and shopping.
Gardening.	House taking.
Cookery.	Benefit Societies.
Travelling.	Annals of gulling.
Housekeeping.	Amusements.
Management of income.	Useful receipts.
Distilling.	Domestic medicines.
Baking.	&c. &c. &c.
Brewing.	

London, printed for Knight and Lacey, 55, Paternoster-Row ; and Westley and Tyrrell, Dublin. M.DCCC.XXV.

A weekly magazine which ran from May 22, 1824, to July 30, 1825. A third volume appeared under the title, ' The Housekeeper's Magazine and Family Economist.'

1825 THE COMPLETE SERVANT ;

being a practical Guide to the peculiar Duties and Business of all Descriptions of Servants, from the Housekeeper to the Servant of all-work, and from the Land Steward to the Foot-Boy ;

With useful Receipts and Tables.

By Samuel and Sarah Adams, fifty years Servants in different Families.

London, published by Knight and Lacey, publishers of books connected with the useful arts, at the James Watt, in Paternoster-Row. M DCCC XXV.

Price Seven Shillings and Sixpence.

There are curious tables as to how many servants should be employed according to different incomes, and the wages to be paid to them. Wages were much lower then than they are now, but board-wages were much the same, viz. ten shillings for women and twelve shillings for men servants.

1825 THE WHOLE ART OF CONFECTIONARY,

comprising sugar boiling, iceing, preserving, candying &c. &c.

According to the Method used by an eminent Confectioner declining Business.

Second edition, improved.

London, printed for Baldwin and Co, Longman and Co, Paternoster-Row; Mozley, Derby; Wilson and Sons, York; Dean, Manchester; Beilby and Knotts, Birmingham; Cullingworth, Leeds; Allardice and Co, Edinburgh; and may be had of all other booksellers.

Price Two Shillings, Boards. 1825.

A thin octavo of 84 pages.

1825 DOMESTIC DUTIES;

or, Instructions to young married ladies, on the management of their households and the regulation of their conduct in the various relations and duties of married life.

By Mrs. William Parkes.

Every wise woman buildeth her house; but the foolish plucketh it down with her hands.

Who can find a virtuous woman? for her price is far above rubies. Her children arise up and call her blessed; her husband also, and he praiseth her. PROVERBS.

London, printed for Longman, Rees, Orme, Brown, and Green, Paternoster-Row. 1825.

The third edition was 1829. There is a half-title.

1825 FRENCH DOMESTIC COOKERY,

combining Economy with Elegance, and adapted to the Use of Families of moderate Fortune.

By an English Physician, many Years resident on the Continent.

London, printed for Thomas Boys, 7, Ludgate-Hill; and Sold by all booksellers. 1825.

An octavo of 418 pages.

158 ENGLISH COOKERY BOOKS

1825 (c.) THE MODERN FAMILY RECEIPT-BOOK, containing a great Variety of Valuable Receipts, arranged under their respective heads, connected with the art of Social and Domestic Life, including many valuable original communications, the result of long experience.

By Mrs. Mary Holland, author of " The Complete Economical Cook ".

London, printed for Thomas Tegg, 73, Cheapside; R. Griffin & Co. Glasgow; R. M. Tims, Dublin; and M. Bandry, Paris.

There is very little about cookery in this book.

1826 THE COOK AND HOUSEWIFE'S MANUAL; containing the most approved modern Receipts for making Soups, Gravies, Sauces, Ragouts, and Made-Dishes; and for Pies, Puddings, Pastry, Pickles, and Preserves:

Also for Baking, Brewing, Making Home-made Wines, Cordials, &c. The whole illustrated by numerous Notes, and practical Observations, on all the various Branches of Domestic Economy.

By Mrs. Margaret Dods, of the Cleikum Inn, St. Ronan's.

—" Cook, see all your sawces
Be sharp and poynant in the palate, that they may
Commend you; look to your roast and baked meats handsomely,
And what new kickshaws and delicate made things."
                                    BEAUMONT AND FLETCHER.

Edinburgh, printed for the author, and sold by Bell & Bradfute, and Oliver & Boyd, Edinburgh; Longman, Rees, Orme, Brown, and Green, London; Robertson & Atkinson, Glasgow; and John Cumming, Dublin. 1826.

A small octavo of 366 pages. There is a half-title. Other editions are 1827 (2), 1829 (4), 1842 (7), 1847 (8), 1854 (10), 1862 (11). Margaret Dods was the landlady in Scott's St. Ronan's Well. The real name of the authoress was Christina Jane Johnstone.

1826 THE ALPHABETICAL RECEIPT BOOK,

and Domestic Adviser, being the only arrangement of the kind ever printed; and forming so complete a Book of reference in all matters of Housekeeping, that any article may in one instant be referred to the same as in a common Dictionary.

Among the innumerable subjects treated upon are

Advice upon	Bleaching	Dress Making
Abdominal Hernia; or Ruptures in the Navel, the Thigh, and the Scrotum.	Botany (Domestic)	Dyeing
	Brewing	Gardening
	Carving	Marketing
	Childbearing	Medicine
Adulterations	Cooking	Perfumery
Agues	Cordial Making	Pickling
Antidotes for Poisons	Culinary Affairs	Preserving
	Distilling	Teething
Asthmas		Wine Making
Baking		Windy Cholic, &c.
Bathing		
Bees, Treatise on		

By Robert Huish Esqr aided by a professional gentleman of the first ability.

London, published by John Williams, 44, Paternoster Row. And may be had of all Booksellers. 1826.

A large octavo of 822 pages with a coloured frontispiece of a lady entitled 'Adjustment of Dress'. The title-page is engraved.

1826 THE CONFECTIONER'S GUIDE,

and Ladies' and Housekeeper's Instructor: being a grand display of pastry, in a variety of forms: also, Confectionary; Iceing, Candying, Preserving, Jelly-Making, Sugar-Boiling, Colouring, &c., &c., in the first of the Art. By James Wallace, late of Philadelphia.

London: printed for the Author, Theobald's Road; and C. Cooper, Leeds. 1826.

A duodecimo of 144 pages.

1826 THE FEMALE'S BEST FRIEND;

or, The Young Woman's Guide to Virtue, Economy, and Happiness: containing a complete modern System of Cookery, formed upon Principles of Economy for Private Families: also

Instructions for Marketing.

The best modes of Trussing, Carving, and Decorating a Table, illustrated by Engravings.

The art of composing the most simple and highly finished Broths, Gravies, Soups, and Sauces.

The mysteries of Potting, Pickling, and Preserving.

The art of making all sorts of Confectionary and Pastry.

Improved methods of making and managing British Wines, also of Brewing and Baking.

Valuable Medicinal Directions, and a great variety of useful Family and Medical Receipts.

To which are added, Instructions to female servants of every description; Advice to the young mother; Rules for the treatment of infants; Directions for nursing, and for the management and education of children; Useful hints for the sick chamber, and for promoting matrimonial happiness:

Illustrated by moral and religious essays, tales, and memoirs of illustrious females, eminent for their piety, virtue, and accomplishments.

The whole being an improved and pleasant Directory for cultivating the Heart and Understanding, and a sure Guide to every acquirement for forming a Pleasing Companion, a Respectable Mother, and a Useful Member of Society.

A new edition, edited and compiled by Watkin Poole, Esq. from writers of unquestionable experience in medicine, cookery, brewing, and every other branch of domestic economy.

Illustrated with beautiful appropriate Engravings.

Manchester, printed and published by J. Gleave and Son, 191, Deansgate. 1826.

A large octavo of 694 pages on the lines of The Young Woman's Companion of 1811 and The Female Instructor of 1815. There is a frontispiece representing a woman and child, with the verse :

> Who gilds my childrens infant day
> With cultivation's dawning ray
> And points to heaven and leads the way ?
> My wife.

There is an engraved title-page. Among the females eminent for piety are Catharine I of Russia and Charlotte Corday. There is a strong denunciation of patent and quack medicines, and a regret 'that we are still inundated with a flood of advertisements in almost every paper ; that the lower and less enlightened classes of the community are still imposed upon by a set of privileged impostors'.

1827 A MODERN SYSTEM OF DOMESTIC COOKERY; or, The Housekeeper's Guide : arranged on the most economical plan for private families. Containing

- The most approved directions for Purchasing, Preserving, and Cooking Butcher's Meat, Fish, Poultry, and Game.
- The best mode of Trussing and Carving.
- The art of composing the most simple and most highly finished Broths, Gravies, Soups, and Sauces.
- The mysteries of Potting and Pickling.
- The art of making all sorts of Confectionary and Pastry.
- An improved method of making British Wines and Cordials.
- Instructions for Brewing and Baking,
- And observations on Culinary Poisons.

A complete Family Physician ; and instructions to female servants in every situation, showing the best methods of performing their various duties.

The whole being the result of actual experiments.

To which are added, as an appendix, some valuable instructions on the management of the kitchen and fruit gardens. By M. Radcliffe.

Manchester, printed and published by J. Gleave and Sons, Top of Market Street, and 191, Deansgate. 1827.

A large octavo of 688 pages with a frontispiece representing 'a domestic scene'. There is an engraved title dated 1822. The book is in large part the same as 'The Female's Best Friend'.

1827 (c.) THE NEW LONDON COOKERY,

and Complete Domestic Guide.

By a lady.

London, published by G. Virtue, 26, Ivy Lane, and Bath Street, Bristol.

> A large octavo of 838 pages with a frontispiece representing a kitchen. 'Hints on Health' contains some excellent advice. 'A habit of taking medicine should be most carefully avoided. 'Great caution should be used in resorting to any advertised medicine. The more wonderful the cure said to be effected by it, the more strongly is it to be suspected. . . . It is the grossest impudence to pretend, and the grossest folly to believe, that one medicine can cure a vast round of diseases.'

1827 DOMESTIC ECONOMY, AND COOKERY,

for rich and poor; containing an account of the best English, Scotch, French, Oriental, and other Foreign Dishes; Preparations of broths and milks for consumption; Receipts for sea-faring men, travellers, and children's food.

Together with estimates and comparisons of dinners and dishes.

The whole composed with the utmost attention to Health, Economy, and Elegance.

By a lady.

London, printed for Longman, Rees, Orme, Brown, and Green, Paternoster-Row. 1827.

> A small octavo of 691 pages.

1829 THE HOUSEKEEPER'S ORACLE;

or, Art of Domestic Management: containing a Complete System of Carving with accuracy and elegance; Hints relative to dinner parties; The art of managing servants; And the economist and epicure's calendar, shewing the seasons when all kinds of meat, fish, poultry, game, vegetables, and fruits.

First arrive in the market—earliest time forced—when most plentiful—and when best and cheapest.
By the late William Kitchiner, M.D.
To which is added a Variety of useful and Original Receipts.
" First for the Kitchen, as without that we shall look lean, and grow faint quickly." HANNAH WOOLEY'S CABINET, 12 mo. 1684, p. 255.
London, printed for Whittaker, Treacher, and Co. Ave Maria Lane. M DCCC XXIX.

There is a portrait of Dr. Kitchiner as preface. The preface is dated from the Albany and signed W. B. Kitchiner.

1829 THE PRACTICE OF COOKERY,
adapted to the business of every day life.
By Mrs. Dalgairns.
Edinburgh, printed for Cadell & Company, Edinburgh; Simpkin and Marshall, London; and all booksellers. 1829.

A small octavo of 528 pages. Other editions are 1835 (3), 1836 (6), and 1849 (11).

1829 THE HOME BOOK ;
or, Young Housekeeper's Assistant : forming a complete system of domestic economy and household accounts.
With estimates of expenditure, &c. &c. in every department of housekeeping, founded on forty-five years personal experience.
By a lady.

" Let these my counsels be a guide to you,
And my experience teach your lack of judgment ;
So shall your Home become a Paradise,
Rich in Earth's purest bliss, Domestic Comfort ! "

London ; Smith, Elder, and Co. 65, Cornhill. 1829.

A thin octavo of 175 pages, written in the form of letters to a young wife.

1829 APICIAN MORSELS;

or, Tales of the Table, Kitchen, and Larder : containing a new and improved code of Eatics ; Select Epicurean Precepts ; Nutritive Maxims, Reflections, Anecdotes, &c.

Illustrating the veritable science of the mouth ; which includes the art of never breakfasting at home, and always dining abroad.

By Dick Humelbergius Secundus.

" O vos qui stomacho laboratis, accurrite, et ego vos restaurabo ! " Vide p. 202.

" Always breakfast as if you did not intend to dine ; and dine as if you had not broken your fast."—CODE GOURMAND.

London : Whittaker, Treacher and Co. Ave-Maria Lane. 1829.

<small>The frontispiece represents a Mr. Eatingtown. There is a half-title. A few recipes are at the end.</small>

1830 THE COOK'S DICTIONARY,

and House-Keeper's Directory : A New Family Manual of Cookery and Confectionary, on a plan of ready reference never hitherto attempted.

By Richard Dolby, cook at the Thatched-House Tavern, St. James's Street.

London : Henry Colburn and Richard Bentley, New Burlington Street. 1830.

<small>A dictionary of 516 pages. There was another edition in 1833.</small>

1830 DOMESTIC ECONOMY.

Vol. I. containing

| Brewing. | Wine-Making. |
| Distilling. | Baking, &c. |

By Michael Donovan Esq. M.R.I.A. professor of chemistry to the company of Apothecaries in Ireland.

London, printed for Longman, Rees, Orme, Brown &

Green, Paternoster Row ; and John Taylor, Upper Gower Street. 1830.

In two volumes. The second volume is on ' human food, animal and vegetable '. The title-page to the two volumes are engraved. The second volume is dated 1837.

1830 (c.) A COLLECTION OF UPWARDS OF 220 RECIPES,
the greater number of which are highly useful, and in daily request in families.
Price one shilling.
Canterbury. Printed and published by S. Prentice, Bookseller and Stationer, Nos. 3 and 20, Guildhall Street.

A pamphlet of 19 pages. The full title is not given as very few of the recipes relate to cookery.

1830 (c.) THE HOUSEWIFE'S GUIDE ;
or, an economical and domestic Art of Cookery, adapted for tradesmen's families ; containing directions for marketing, relative to the choice and purchase of beef, butter, eggs, cheese, bacon, hams, fowls, ducks, geese, fish, mutton, lamb, pork, veal, &c. &c.
Also instructions for dressing butchers' meat, poultry, game, fish, &c.
Likewise for preparing soups, broths, gravies, and sauces ; with the different branches of pastry and confectionary.
To which is added, The art of potting, collaring, pickling, and preserving ; Directions for carving, and approved receipts for made wines.
By Mrs. Deborah Irwin, twenty-three years cook to a tradesman with a large family.
London, printed and published by William Mason, 22 Clerkenwell Green.
One Shilling.

A pamphlet of 72 pages. A frontispiece illustrates the art of carving.

1830 THE COMPLETE ECONOMICAL COOK

and Frugal Housewife : an entire new System of Domestic Cookery, containing approved directions for purchasing, preserving, and cooking.

Also, trussing & carving ; preparing soups, gravies, sauces, made dishes, potting, pickling, &c. with directions for pastry and confectionary.

Likewise the art of making British wines, brewing, baking, gardening, &c.

By Mrs. Mary Holland, professed cook.

" I had rather you would marry a Young Woman without a Farthing, who is mistress of the art of Domestic Economy, than one who has Ten Thousand Pounds, and unacquainted with that necessary appendage to a good Wife."

Dr. Johnson.

The sixth edition, considerably amended and enlarged, the result of thirty years' practice.

London, printed for Thomas Tegg, 73, Cheapside ; Simpkin and Marshall ; Sherwood, Jones and Co. Also R. Griffin and Co. Glasgow ; and J. Cumming, Dublin. 1830.

A duodecimo of 288 pages with a frontispiece representing a kitchen. There is also an engraved title. On the cover the book is called the seventh edition. It is apparently a later edition of 'The Complete British Cook' of 1800.

1830 (c.) KIDD'S PRACTICAL HINTS

for the use of young carvers ; with thirty-nine engravings.

" What then shall be said for our modern 'Whipper-Snappers', who professing to know everything, are yet ignorant of the *divine* art of Carving ; and are obliged to confess, amidst the ridicule of their friends, that they know nothing whatever about it ? " Sharpe's Gastronomical Essaies. 1801.

London, published for W. Kidd, by W. Ingham, 14, Chandos Street, Strand ; and sold by all booksellers.

A duodecimo of 33 pages with a frontispiece representing four men at dinner.

There is a corresponding volume called 'Kidd's Instructions in Fashionable Cookery'.

1831 A NEW SYSTEM OF PRACTICAL DOMESTIC ECONOMY ;

founded on modern discoveries, and the private communications of persons of experience.

New edition, revised and enlarged ; with estimates of household expenses, adapted to families of every description.

In every point of view, an Economist is a good character.—
HUNTER's CULINA.

London : Colburn and Bentley, New Burlington Street. 1831.

An octavo of 463 pages. There is a half-title.

1833 VEGETABLE COOKERY ;
with an introduction, recommending abstinence from animal food and intoxicating liquors.

By a lady.

The fourth edition.

London, published by Effingham Wilson, Royal Exchange ; Messrs. Clarke, and Messrs. Thomson, Manchester ; F. W. Wakeman, Dublin ; and Messrs. Waugh and Innes, Edinburgh. M DCCC XXXIII.

A duodecimo of 451 pages. There is an engraved title.

1833 THE HOUSEWIFE'S GUIDE :
or a Complete System of Modern Cookery, particularly adapted to the Middle Class of Society, and diligently selected from the most approved Works.

Belfast, printed by Joseph Smyth, High Street. 1833.

A pamphlet of 144 pages.

1834 THE HOUSEKEEPER'S GUIDE,
or a plain and practical system of Domestic cookery.
By Esther Copley, author of Cottage Comforts &c.

London, printed for Jackson & Walford. 18. S^t. Pauls Church Yard. 1834.

The author's name is not on the title-page but on an engraved title. The frontispiece represents a larder. The book is a small octavo of 407 pages.

1834 THE ROYAL PARISIAN PASTRY COOK,
translated from the original of M. A. Carême by John Porter.

I have not been able to find this book. The B.M. copy has been missing since 1877, but the entry still remains in the catalogue.

1835 ELEMENTS OF THE ARTS OF COOKERY AND CONFECTIONARY.
By Mrs. M'Ewan.
Edinburgh. 1835.

I have not been able to find a copy of this book.

1835 THE FRUGAL HOUSEWIFE,
dedicated to those who are not ashamed of economy.
By Mrs. Child, author of the " Mother's book ", the " Little Girl's Book ", the " Mother's Story Book ", &c.

A fat kitchen maketh a lean will. FRANKLIN.

" Economy is a poor man's revenue ; extravagance a rich man's ruin."

Fifteenth edition, corrected and arranged by the author.
To which are added hints to persons of moderate fortune.
Also, by the English editor, Some valuable domestic receipts, &c.
London, printed for T. Tegg and Son, Cheapside ; N. Hailes, Piccadilly ; Bowdery and Kerby, Oxford Street ; R. Griffin and Co. Glasgow ; and Tegg, Wise, and Co. Dublin. 1835.

A little book of 176 pages with a lady and her cook as frontispiece.

1836 THE YOUNG COOK'S GUIDE;

with practical observations. A new treatise on French and English cookery, combining economy with elegance.

By I. Roberts, cook to his late Royal Highness the Duke of Gloucester, the late Right Hon. Earl of Clarendon, the Right Hon. Lord Dynevor, and now to the present Right Hon. Earl of Clarendon.

To which is added an Appendix, containing M. Appert's method of preserving fruit without sugar. The rudiments of ices, and many useful performances in the art of confectionary.

London: published by Laking, stationer to her Royal Highness the Duchess of Gloucester, Curzon Street, May Fair. 1836.

A large octavo of 307 pages. There is an imposing list of subscribers headed by the Duchess of Gloucester and the Princess Sophia Matilda.

1836-1844 THE MAGAZINE OF DOMESTIC ECONOMY.

Volume the first.

We are born at home, we live at home, and we must die at home, so that the comfort and economy of home are of more deep, heart-felt, and personal interest to us, than the public affairs of all the nations in the world.

London, published by Orr and Smith, Paternoster Row; and W. & R. Chambers, Edinburgh. M DCCC XXXVI.

A monthly magazine full of information about cookery.

1836 FRENCH COOKERY:

comprising *L'Art de la cuisine française; Le Pâtissier royal; Le Cuisinier parisien*

By the late M. Carême, some time chef of the kitchen of His Majesty George IV.

Translated by William Hall, cook to T. P. Williams, Esq., M.P., and conductor of the parliamentary dinners of the

Right Honourable Lord Viscount Canterbury, G.C.B., late speaker of the House of Commons.
With Seventy-three plates illustrative of the art.
London: John Murray, Albemarle Street. MDCCCXXXVI.

<small>A large octavo of 422 pages. The author says in his preface that he began the translation some years before Porter produced his edition, and begs 'to disclaim being actuated by any rivalry'</small>

1838 THE HOUSEWIFE'S GUIDE,
or, a complete system of modern cookery; containing directions how to roast and boil every thing necessary for the Table; To cure hams, bacon, &c.; How to make gravies, sauces, fricasees, and various Dishes for Lent: particularly adapted for the middle class of society.
By a lady.
Otley, printed by William Walker, Kirkgate. 1838.
Price One Shilling.

<small>A pamphlet of 48 pages.</small>

1838 (c.) WALKER'S NEW FAMILY RECEIPT-BOOK;
containing valuable secrets in the preparation of the most useful articles in Domestic Economy, compiled from respectable sources of information, and given in plain and intelligible language, which all may understand.
Otley, printed by William Walker, Sold by all booksellers.
Price one shilling and six pence.

<small>A pamphlet of 72 pages.</small>

1838 THE GENERAL RECEIPT-BOOK,
containing an extensive collection of valuable receipts, connected with Domestic Economy.
By James W. Laughton.
Ninetieth edition.
London, printed & published by William Mason, 22, Clerkenwell Green.
Six-Pence. 1838.

<small>A pamphlet of 23 pages with a few cookery recipes. The 105th edition is 1843.</small>

1838 SECOND COLLECTION. THE GENERAL RECEIPT-BOOK,

containing near two hundred of the most useful receipts, connected with Domestic Economy, Cookery, Confectionery, Chymistry, the Arts and Sciences, &c. &c.

Edited by James W. Laughton.

London, printed & published by William Mason, 22, Clerkenwell Green.

Sixpence.

A pamphlet of 48 pages. The price of the second edition (1838) was eightpence. The preface states that over 300,000 copies were sold of the first collection.

1838 HINTS FOR THE TABLE :

or, The Economy of Good Living.

> To form a science and a nomenclature
> From out the commonest demands of nature.
>
> BYRON.

London : Simpkin, Marshall, and Co. Stationers' Hall Court. 1838.

A duodecimo of 167 pages. There is a half-title. The book is full of interesting facts and stories.

1841-3 THE EPICURE'S ALMANAC ;

or Diary of good living ; containing a choice and original receipt or a valuable hint for every day in the year.

The result of actual experience, applicable to the enjoyment of the good things of this life, consistently with the views of those who study genteel economy.

By Benson E. Hill, author of " Recollections of an artillery officer ", " A pinch of snuff ", &c. &c.

> " Pan *shall* remain."—MIDAS.

London : How and Parsons, 132, Fleet Street. 1841.

A duodecimo which was published in the years 1841, 1842, and 1843. There is a half-title to each volume. There is an account of the author by W. P. Courtney in Notes and Queries for March 4, 1905.

172 ENGLISH COOKERY BOOKS

1841 (*c.*) THE BISCUIT-BAKER'S AND PASTRY-COOK'S ASSISTANT;

containing upwards of one hundred receipts, for making all kinds of biscuits, pastry, gingerbread, &c. &c.

By Thomas Shoesmith, Pastry-Cook and Biscuit-Baker.

Fourth edition, corrected and improved.

London: Dean and Munday, Threadneedle-Street.

Price One Shilling.

A pamphlet of 72 pages.

1842 THE HOUSEWIFE'S GUIDE;

or, A new system of plain economical cookery, containing directions how to roast and boil every thing necessary for the table, To cure hams and bacon, &c. How to make gravies, sauces, fricassees, pies, tarts, & pastes, pickling and preserving. Particularly adapted to the middle class of society.

By Mrs. Robinson.

Bath, printed for Mrs. Robinson. 1842.

Price One Shilling.

A pamphlet of 60 pages with a frontispiece to illustrate the art of carving. Many of the recipes are copied from the book with the same title published at Otley in 1838.

1842 THE GUIDE TO TRADE. THE CONFECTIONER:

containing the method of making all sorts of preserves, sugar-boiling, comfit making, lozenges, ornamental cakes, ices, liqueurs, waters, and gum-paste ornaments.

By George Read.

London: Charles Knight and Co., Ludgate Street. 1842.

A duodecimo of 148 pages.

1842 (*c.*) THE PASTRY-COOK'S AND CONFECTIONER'S ASSISTANT:

containing the most approved and choice receipts for making all manner of pastry, patties, tarts, pies, puddings, jellies, blanc-manges, and creams.

With directions for making bride-cakes, savoy, sponge, almond, ratafia and rout cakes; Macaroons, rock, and other biscuits; Buns, Bath buns, and tea cakes; The best methods of preserving fruit; The art of sugar boiling, making lozenges, drops, pipe, barley-sugar, twist, carraway comfits, &c.
As practised at the principal establishments in London.
By George Read, Confectioner and pastry-cook.
London: Dean and Munday, Threadneedle-Street.

[1s. 6d.]

A little book of 82 pages. The sixth edition is called 'The Confectioner's and Pastry-cook's Guide'.

1843 (c.) THE COMPLETE BISCUIT AND GINGER-BREAD BAKER'S ASSISTANT:
containing the most approved methods, with practical directions, for making all manner of plain and fancy biscuits, buns, cakes, drops, thick gingerbread, spice nuts, &c.
Being adapted either for the use of the trade or private families.
The only work exclusively on this subject extant.
Forming the second part of "The confectioner's and pastry-cook's guide".
By George Read, author of "The confectioner", "The confectioner's and pastry-cook's guide", and "The practical baker".
London: Dean and Co. Threadneedle Street, and Cleave, Shoe-Lane.

Price 2s. 6d.

112 pages.

1843 FISH,
how to choose and how to dress.
By Piscator, author of "The Practical Angler", &c., &c.
London: Longman, Brown, Green, and Longmans. 1843.

A duodecimo of 296 pages. 'A Practical Treatise on the Choice and Cookery of Fish,' by Piscator (Second edition. London: Longman, Brown, Green, and Longmans. 1854), is apparently the second and revised edition.

1844 COTTAGE ECONOMY AND COOKERY.
London, printed by William Clowes and Sons, Stamford Street. 1844.

A pamphlet of 20 pages, compiled by French Burke, Esq., from essays submitted to the Royal Agricultural Society of England; and reprinted from the Journal of the Society, 1842, vol. iii, part I.

1844 THE ICE BOOK :
being a compendious and concise history of everything connected with Ice from its first introduction into Europe as an article of luxury to the present time ;
With an account of the artificial manner of producing pure & solid ice, and a valuable collection of the most approved recipes for making superior water ices and ice creams at a few minutes' notice.
By Thomas Masters.

> "Tut ! tut ! thou art all ice,
>   Thy kindness freezes."
>   RICHARD III.—Act IV. Scene 2.

London : Simpkin, Marshall, & Co., Stationers' Hall Court, Ludgate Street. 1844.

A large octavo of 198 pages. There is a half-title. The same author published in 1850 'A Short Treatise concerning some Patent Inventions and Apparatus for the Production of Ice, &c., &c.', which gives recipes for ices.

1844 AN ENCYCLOPÆDIA OF DOMESTIC ECONOMY :
comprising such subjects as are most immediately connected with housekeeping : as, The construction of domestic edifices, with the modes of warming, ventilating, and lighting them ; A description of the various articles of furniture, with the nature of their materials ; Duties of servants ; A general account of the animal and vegetable substances used as food, and the methods of preserving and preparing them by cooking ; Making bread ; The chemical nature and the preparation of all kinds of fermented liquors used

ENGLISH COOKERY BOOKS

as beverage ; Materials employed in dress and the toilette ; Business of the laundry ; Description of the various wheel-carriages ; Preservation of health ; Domestic medicine, &c. &c.

By Thomas Webster, F.G.S., &c. assisted by the late Mrs. Parkes, author of " Domestic Duties."

Illustrated with nearly one thousand woodcuts.

London : Longman, Brown, Green, and Longmans, Paternoster-Row. 1844.

A large volume of 1264 pages.

1844 INSTRUCTIONS IN HOUSEHOLD MATTERS ;
or, The young girl's guide to domestic service.

Written by a lady, with an especial view to young girls intended for service on leaving school.

London : John W. Parker, West Strand. M DCCC XLIV.

A little book of 124 pages with a frontispiece representing an American organ.

1845 MODERN COOKERY
in all its branches : reduced to a system of easy practice, for the use of private families.

In a series of practical receipts, which have been strictly tested, and are given with the most minute exactness.

By Eliza Acton.

Illustrated with numerous woodcuts.

London : Longman, Brown, Green and Longmans, Paternoster Row. 1845.

A duodecimo of 683 pages. There is a half-title. Other editions are 1845 (2), 1846 (5), 1855.

1845 (c.) COOKERY MADE EASY ;
or, The most plain and practical directions for properly cooking and serving-up all sorts of provisions, from a single joint of meat, with vegetables, to the most exquisitely-seasoned dishes of poultry, fish, and game,

Every necessary direction being clearly described in the most exact and accurate manner, whether for steaming, boiling, roasting, baking, frying, broiling, stewing, hashing, or mincing :

Also the proper methods of making plain & rich gravies, sauces, soups, broths, &c.

To which are added, plain and practical directions for making, and for properly cooking pies, puddings, tarts, patties, custards, & other pastry, and for pickling, making ketchups, &c.

The whole written entirely from practice, and combining gentility with economy.

By a lady.

Third edition, improved.

London, published by Dean and Co. Threadneedle-Street.

A little book of 172 pages with a frontispiece representing the art of trussing. Other editions are 1850 (8) and 1875 (21).

1846 THE JEWISH MANUAL ;

or practical information in Jewish and modern cookery, with a collection of valuable recipes & hints relating to the toilette.

Edited by a lady.

London : T. & W. Boone, 29, New Bond Street. 1846.

A book of 244 pages, apparently the first of its kind.

1846 THE GASTRONOMIC REGENERATOR :

a simplified and entirely new System of Cookery, with nearly two thousand practical receipts suited to the income of all classes.

Illustrated with numerous engravings and correct and minute plans how kitchens of every size, from the kitchen of a royal palace to that of the humble cottage, are to be constructed and furnished.

By Monsieur A. Soyer, of the Reform Club.

London : Simpkin, Marshall, & Co., Stationers' Hall Court ; and sold by John Ollivier, Pall-Mall. 1846.

A portrait of the author as frontispiece and an engraved title. Other editions are 1849 (6) and 1852.

1846 FRENCH DOMESTIC COOKERY,

combining elegance with economy ; describing new culinary implements and processes ; the management of the table ; instructions for carving ; French, German, Polish, Spanish, and Italian Cookery :

In twelve hundred receipts.

Besides a variety of new modes of keeping and storing provisions, domestic hints, &c. management of wines, &c. With many engravings.

London : David Boyne, Fleet Street. M DCCC XLVI.

This is an adapted translation of *La cuisinière de la Campagne et de la Ville*.

1846 THE MODERN COOK,

a practical guide to the culinary art in all its branches, adapted as well for the largest establishments, as for the use of private families.

By Charles Elmé Francatelli, pupil of the celebrated Careme, and late maître d'hotel and chief cook to Her Majesty the Queen.

With illustrations.

London : Richard Bentley, New Burlington Street, publisher in ordinary to Her Majesty. 1846.

A portrait of the author as frontispiece. Other editions are 1853 (8) and 1855 (9).

1847 THE WHOLE ART OF CURING,

pickling, and smoking meat and fish, both in the British and foreign modes ; with many useful miscellaneous receipts, and full directions for the construction of an

economical drying-chimney and apparatus, on an entirely original plan.
By James Robinson, eighteen years a practical curer.
London, printed for Longman, Brown, Green, and Longmans, Paternoster-Row. 1847.

A little book of 153 pages.

1847 A FEW RECIPES OF VEGETARIAN DIET;
with suggestions for the formation of a dietary from which the flesh of animals is excluded;
Accompanied by scientific facts, showing that vegetable food is more nutritive, and more digestible than the flesh of animals.
London: Whittaker & Co., Ave-Maria Lane. 1847.

A pamphlet of 39 pages.

1847 (c.) THE FOOTMAN'S GUIDE:
containing plain instructions for the footman and butler, for the proper arrangement and regular performance of their various duties, in large or small families:
Including the manner of setting-out tables, sideboards, &c. &c. The art of waiting at table, and superintending large and small breakfast, dinner, and supper parties; Directions for cleaning and preserving plate, glass, furniture, clothes, &c. and for delivering and receiving cards and messages; And other useful information.
Fourth edition, embellished with appropriate plates, and bills of fare.
By James Williams.
London: Thomas Dean and Co. Threadneedle-Street.

An interesting book, full of detailed information on all duties of a footman, e.g. 'Should you have to carry a cane when walking out, hold it two-thirds of the way up; let the large end of the cane be uppermost; but if you are riding behind a carriage with it, let the small end be uppermost.'

1848 (*c.*) CHARITABLE COOKERY ;
or, The poor man's regenerator.
By A. Soyer, of the Reform Club, London.
London : Simpkin, Marshall, and Co. and John Ollivier.
Dublin : Hodges and Smith, Grafton Street.
Price Sixpence.

A pamphlet of 50 pages.

1849 THE FINCHLEY MANUALS OF INDUSTRY.
No. I. Cooking ; or, Practical and economical training for those who are to be servants, wives, or mothers.
Management of the kitchen, plain cooking, bread-making, baking, brewing, pickling, &c.
Prepared for the use of the national and industrial schools of the Holy Trinity, at Finchley.
London : Joseph Masters, Aldersgate Street, and 78, New Bond Street. M DCCC XLIX.

A duodecimo of 142 pages.

No. III. Household work ; or, The duties of female servants, practically and economically illustrated, through the respective grades of maid-of-all work, house and parlour-maid, and laundry-maid.
With many valuable recipes for facilitating labour in every department. M DCCC L.

A duodecimo of 110 pages in the form of question and answer.

1849 (*c.*) THE COOK.
Plain and practical directions for cooking and housekeeping ; with upwards of 700 receipts.
By W. G. Lewis.
A new edition, corrected and improved, by G. Read.
London : Houlston and Stoneman, 65, Paternoster Row.

An octavo of 332 pages.

1849 THE MODERN HOUSEWIFE
or Ménagère, comprising nearly one thousand receipts for the economic and judicious preparation of every meal of the day, with those of the nursery and sick room, and minute directions for family management in all its branches. Illustrated with engravings, including the modern housewife's unique kitchen, and magic stove.
By Alexis Soyer, author of " The gastronomic regenerator ",
(Reform Club)
London : Simpkin, Marshall, & Co., Stationers' Hall Court ; Ollivier, Pall Mall. 1849.

There is a frontispiece of the author, and after the title-page is an engraved dedication. The thirtieth thousand was published in 1853.

1850 COMMON SENSE FOR HOUSEMAIDS.
By a lady.
London : J. Hatchard and Son, 187, Piccadilly. 1850.

A little book of 100 pages. There was a second edition in 1853.

ADDENDUM

1712 THE UNIVERSAL LIBRARY ;
or, Compleat Summary of Science. Containing above sixty select treatises.
In two volumes.
I. Of Theology, . . . Cookery and Dyet.
II. Of Animals, . . .
With divers Secrets, Experiments and Curiosities therein.
London : printed for George Sambridge at the Three Flower-de-Lys in Little Britain. 1712.

The cookery portion is in vol. i, pp. 553–68. The preface is signed H. Curzon. The authorities given for this subject are : The Accomplish'd Lady's Delight, Royal Cookery, Howard's Cookery, Lamb's Cookery, May's Cookery, The Queen-like Closet by Hannah Wolley.

APPENDIX

The following is a list of some books published after 1850. They are not included in the Index.

1851. Modern Domestic Cookery, by a lady.
1852. Indian Domestic Cookery, third edition.
                1860 (5), 1865 (6).
1852. The Illustrated London Cookery Book, by Frederick Bishop.
1852 (c.). Gentility and Economy combined, by George Read.
1853. The Pantropheon, by Alexis Soyer.
1853. French Cookery, by Miss Crawford.
1853. French Confectionary, by Miss Crawford.
      This was joined to the preceding book in the third edition (1855).
1853 (c.). The Manual of French Cookery.
1854. Modern Household Cookery, by a lady.
1854. New Household Receipt-book, by Mrs. Sarah Hale.
1854. The Art of Good and Cheap Cookery.
                A pamphlet of 40 pages.
1854 (c.). The Art of Catering and Carving.
1854 (c.). Plain Family Recipes.
                A pamphlet of 24 pages.
1855. A Shilling Cookery for the People, by Alexis Soyer.
1855. The Pocket Guide to Domestic Cookery. (Glasgow.)
1857. Culinary Campaign, by Alexis Soyer.
1857. Every Lady her own Cook, by a lady.
                A pamphlet of 19 pages.
1860. Instructions to Military Hospital Cooks.
                    Recipes by A. Soyer.

APPENDIX

1860. The Art of Carving made Easy. (Glasgow.)
1861. The Cook's Guide, by C. E. Francatelli.
1861. The Lady's Guide, by a lady.
1861 (c.). My Receipt Book, by a lady.
1862. The Royal English and French Confectioner, by C. E. Francatelli.
1862 (c.). A Plain Cookery Book for the Working Classes, by C. E. Francatelli.
1867. Good Cookery Illustrated, by the Right Hon. Lady Llanover.
1869. Memoirs of Alexis Soyer with unpublished receipts, by F. Volant and J. R. Warren.
1869 (c.). The Indian Cookery Book.
                Another edition in 1880.
1870. Artistic Cookery, by Urbain Dubois.
1870. Cosmopolitan Cookery, by Urbain Dubois.
1871. The Household Cookery Book, by Urbain Dubois.

INDEX OF AUTHORS

Abbot, Robert, 126.
Accum, Frederick, 151.
Acton, Eliza, 175.
Adams, Samuel and Sarah, 156.
Alcock, Elizabeth, 141.
Alexis of Piedmont, 3.
Anguilbert, Theobald, 15.
Apicius Coelius, 49.
Appert, F., 141.
Armstrong, John, 74.
Arnaldus de Villa Nova, 14.
Arnand, J., 71.
Ashburn, Addison, 135.
Atkyns, Arabella, 72.

B., M., 21.
B., N., 37.
B., W., 15.
Bailey, N., 54, 69.
Barker, Anne, 94.
Bate, John, 20.
Battam, Anne, 80.
Beauvilliers, A. B., 155.
Bennett, Christopher, 27.
Boorde, Andrew, 4.
Borella, 102.
Bradley, Martha, 105.
Bradley, Richard, 58, 59.
Brand, H. W., 135.
Briggs, Richard, 116.
Brooks, Catharine, 93.
Burke, French, 174.
Busk, Hans, 147.
Butler, Caroline, 103.
Buttes, Henry, 12.

C., R., 37.
Caird, J., 137.
Carême, M. A., 168, 169.
Carter, Charles, 61, 62, 77.
Carter, Susannah, 122.
Carter, W., 126.
Chambers, Amelia, 128.
Child, Mrs., 168.
Chomel, N., 58.
Cleland, Elizabeth, 88.

Clements, 155.
Clermont, B., 101.
Cocchi, A., 76.
Cochrane, James, 150.
Cocke, Thomas, 39.
Cole, Mary, 118.
Collingwood, Francis, 121.
Cook, Ann, 91.
Cooke, J. C., 154.
Cooper, Joseph, 25.
Copley, Esther, 167.
Cosnett, Thomas, 153.
Crell, A. F., 155.
Cromwell, Elizabeth, 33.
Curzon, H., 181.

Dalgairns, Mrs., 163.
Dalrymple, George, 113.
Dawson, Thomas, 7.
Dickinson, Francisco, 22.
Digby, Sir Kenelm, 34.
Dods, Margaret, 158.
Dolby, Richard, 164.
Donat, Mrs., 134.
Donovan, Michael, 164.

Eales, Mary, 55.
Eaton, Mary, 153.
Ellis, W., 79.
Elyot, Sir Thomas, 2.
Evelyn, John, 46.

Fairfax, Arabella, 85.
Farley, John, 114, 124.
Fisher, George, 74.
Fisher, Mrs., 82.
Francatelli, C. E., 177.
Frazer, Mrs., 120.

G., I. D., 24.
Gelleroy, William, 92.
Glasse, A., 125.
Glasse, Elizabeth, 110.
Glasse, Hannah, 77, 90, 91, 131.
Gratarolus, Gulielmus, 5.
Grey, Elizabeth, 23.

INDEX OF AUTHORS

H., J., 46.
H., M., 43.
Hall, T., 52.
Hall, William, 169.
Hammond, Elizabeth, 144.
Harrison, Sarah, 64.
Hart, James, 20.
Hartman, George, 34, 41.
Haselmore, Anthony, 155.
Haslehurst, Priscilla, 132.
Hay, D., 48.
Hazlemore, Maximilian, 122.
Henderson, W. A., 134.
Hester, John, 6.
Hill, Benson E., 171.
Holland, Mary, 127, 158, 166.
Howard, Henry, 51.
Hudson, Mrs., 134.
Hughson, D., 145.
Huish, Robert, 159.
Humelbergius, Dick, 164.
Hunter, A., 133.

Ignotus, 133.
Irwin, Deborah, 165.

J., W., 22.
Jackson, Sarah, 86.
Jarrin, G. A., 149.
Jenks, James, 98.
Jennings, James, 151.
Johnson, Mary, 83.
Johnstone, Christina J., 158.

K., J., 48.
K., T., 9.
Kent, Countess of, 23.
Kidder, E., 71.
King, W., 51.
Kitchiner, W., 146, 163.
Kittelby, Mary, 54.

La Chapelle, V., 63.
La Fountaine, 22.
Lamb, Patrick, 53.
Lambert, Edward, 81.
Laughton, James W., 170, 171.
La Varenne, 24.
Lemery, Louis, 48.
Lemery, N., 53.
Lessius, Leonard, 20.
Lewis, W. G., 179.
Lister, Martin, 49.
Lupton, Thomas, 12.

M., W., 26.
Macdonald, Duncan, 129.
M'Ewan, Mrs., 168.
Maciver, Mrs., 106.
Mackenzie, Colin, 152.
Macquin, A.-D., 148.
Markham, Gervase, 16.
Marnette, 28.
Marshall, Elizabeth, 108.
Martin, Sarah, 123.
Mason, Charlotte, 107-8.
Massiolot, 48.
Masters, Thomas, 174.
May, Robert, 30.
Mayerne, Sir Theodore, 29.
Melroe, Eliza, 125.
Menon, 101.
Middleton, John, 64.
Millington, Charles, 138.
Mollard, John, 131.
Morris, Mary, 64.
Moxon, Elizabeth, 78.
Muffett, Thomas, 27.
Murrell, John, 16, 17, 19.

Newton, J. F., 141.
Newton, Thomas, 5, 8.
Nott, John, 57.
Nourse, Mrs., 148.
Nutt, Frederick, 117, 136.

Onesimus, 153.

P., J., 37.
P., T., 37, 38.
Papin, Denys, 40, 41.
Parkes, Mrs., 157, 175.
Partridge, Ann, 111.
Partridge, John, 4.
Paynell, T., 14.
Peckham, Ann, 96.
Pegge, Samuel, 109.
Perkins, John, 119.
Philotheus Physiologus, 43.
Phioravante, Leonardo, 6.
'Piscator', 173.
Plat, H., 13.
Plumptre, Arabella, 139.
Poole, Watkin, 160.
Porter, John, 168.
Powell, 130.
Price, Elizabeth, 109, 110.

INDEX OF AUTHORS

R., C., 50.
R., M., 11.
Rabisha, William, 31.
Radcliffe, M., 161.
Raffald, Elizabeth, 94, 99.
Read, George, 172, 173.
Ritson, Joseph, 132.
Roberts, I., 169.
Robertson, Hannah, 97.
Robinson, James, 178.
Robinson, Mrs., 172.
Rose, Giles, 42.
Rosselli, G. de, 12.
Rundle, Mrs., 136, 137.
Ruthven, Lord, 21.

St. Clouet, 89.
Salmon, William, 46.
Schnebbelie, J. C., 134.
Scott, Sir Michael, 15.
Shackleford, Ann, 95.
Shewring, Adam, 39.
Shirley, John, 44.
Shoesmith, Thomas, 172.
Simpson, John, 135.
Skeat, J., 100.
Slack, Mrs., 74.
Smith, Elizabeth, 60.
Smith, Mary, 106.
Smith, Mrs., 138.
Smith, R., 55.
Smith, Timothy, 20.
Soyer, A., 177, 179, 180.

Strangehopes, Samuel, 32.
Sturgeon, Launcelot, 151.

Tasso, Torquato, 9.
Taylor, E., 100.
Thacker, John, 88.
Tillinghast, Mary, 40.
Trusler, J., 117.
Tryon, Thomas, 37, 43.
Turswell, Thomas, 7.
Twyne, Thomas, 7.

Ude, L. E., 142.

Vaughan, William, 13.
Venner, Tobias, 18.
Verral, William, 89.

W., A., 9.
W., J., 50.
Wallace, James, 159.
Wallace, W. M., 155.
Ward, William, 4.
Warner, Richard, 120.
Webster, Thomas, 175.
Westcott, Mrs., 146.
Williams, James, 178.
Williams, T., 124.
Willis, Michael, 154.
Wilson, Maria, 91.
Winter, Salvator, 22.
Woollams, John, 121.
Woolley, Hannah, 31, 32, 35, 36.

INDEX OF TITLES

Accomplisht cook, 29.
Accomplished family cook, 124.
Accomplished housekeeper and universal cook, 123.
Accomplish'd housewife, 75.
Accomplish'd housewife and housekeeper's pocket companion, 68.
Accomplished ladies rich closet of rarities, 43.
Accomplish'd lady's delight, 37.
Accomplished lady's delight in cookery, 112.
Acetaria, 46.
Adam's luxury and Eve's cookery, 74.
Alarm to all persons, 70.
Alphabetical receipt book, 159.
Antiquitates culinariæ, 120.
Apician morsels, 164.
Apicius redevivus, 145.
Archimagirus anglo-gallicus, 29.
Art of confectionary, 81.
Art of cookery, 25, 51, 88.
Art of cookery and pastery, 99.
Art of cookery made easy and refined, 130.
Art of cookery made plain and easy, 76, 131.
Art of French cookery, 155.
Art of invigorating and prolonging life, 146.
Art of modern cookery displayed, 95.
Art of preserving, 141.
Art of preserving health, 74.

Banquet, 146.
Beauties treasury, 50.
Biscuit-baker's and pastry-cook's assistant, 172.
Boke of cokery, 1.
Boke of kervynge, 1.
Book of cookrye, 9.
Book of fruits and flowers, 24.
Book of knowledge, 32.

Booke of carving and serving, 2, 8, 19.
Booke of carvyng, 2, 8.
Booke of cookerie, 10, 18.
British housewife, 104, 139.
British jewel, 112.

Castel of helthe, 2.
Charitable cookery, 179.
Choice and experimental receipts, 34.
Choice collection of cookery receipts, 107.
Choice manuall, 22.
Closet for ladies and gentlewomen, 14.
Closet of the eminently learned Sir Kenelme Digby, 34.
Collection of above three hundred receipts, 54.
Collection of one hundred and thirty-seven approved receipts, 107.
Collection of ordinances and regulations, 119.
Collection of scarce and valuable receipts, 80.
Collection of upwards of 220 recipes, 165.
Common sense for housemaids, 180.
Compedyous regyment, 4.
Compendium of the rationall secretes, 6.
Compleat city and country cook, 62.
Compleat confectioner, 54-5.
Compleat cook, 26, 27, 37.
Compleat English and French cook, 37.
Compleat gentlewoman, 36.
Compleat housewife, 60.
Compleat servant-maid, 39.
Complete biscuit and gingerbread baker's assistant, 173.
Complete British cook, 127.

INDEX OF TITLES

Complete confectioner, 90, 117.
Complete confectioner and family cook, 137.
Complete cook, 97.
Complete economical cook, 166.
Complete English cook, 93, 95.
Complete family-piece, 66.
Complete house-keeper and professed cook, 106.
Complete practical cook, 61.
Complete servant, 156.
Complete servant maid, 94.
Complete system of cookery, 89, 134.
Confectioner's and pastry-cook's guide, 173.
Confectioner's guide, 159.
Cook, 179.
Cook and confectioner's guide, 126.
Cook and housekeeper's complete and universal dictionary, 152.
Cook and housewife's manual, 158.
Cookery (Nourse), 148.
Cookery and confectionary, 154.
Cookery and pastry, 106.
Cookery made easy, 154, 175.
Cookery reformed, 86.
Cook's and confectioner's dictionary, 56.
Cook's dictionary, 164.
Cooks guide, 32.
Cook's oracle, 145.
Cottage economy and cookery, 174.
Country housewife and lady's director, 58.
Country housewife's family companion, 79.
Court and country confectioner, 102.
Court and country cook, 47.
Court and kitchin of Elizabeth Cromwell, 33.
Court cookery, 55.
Culina famulatrix medicinæ, 133.
Culinary chemistry, 150.

Daily exercise for ladies and gentlewomen, 16.
Delightes for ladies, 13.

Delightfull daily exercise, 18.
De opsoniis et condimentis, 49.
Dessert, 147.
Dictionaire oeconomique, 57.
Dictionarium domesticum, 69.
Dictionarium rusticum, 54.
Direction for the health of magistrates, 5.
Director, 86.
Domestic duties, 157.
Domestic economy, 122, 164.
Domestic economy and cookery, 162.
Domestic management, 128, 139.
Dyets dry dinner, 12.

Economical and new method of cookery, 125.
Economical cookery, 154.
Economist, 155.
Economist and general adviser, 156.
Elements of the arts of cookery and confectionary, 168.
Encyclopædia of domestic economy, 174.
Englands newest way, 51.
English and French cook, 37.
English art of cookery, 115.
English housewifery, 78.
English hus-wife, 15.
Englishman's docter, 14.
Epicure's almanac, 142, 171.
Epulario, 12.
Essay on abstinence from animal food, 132.
Essays, moral, philosophical, and stomachical, 151.
Experienced English housekeeper, 98.

Family cyclopædia, 151.
Family dictionary, 45.
Family director, 135.
Family friend, 132.
Family magazine, 71.
Family oracle, 155.
Family receipt book, 144, 146.
Family's best friend, 85.
Farmer's wife, 111.
Female economist, 138.
Female instructor, 143.
Female's best friend, 160.

INDEX OF TITLES

Few recipes of vegetarian diet, 178.
Finchley manuals of industry, 179.
Fish, 173.
Five hundred new receipts, 64.
Five thousand receipts, 152.
Footman's directory, 153.
Footman's guide, 178.
Forme of cury, 108.
French and English cooke, 29.
French cook, 23, 142.
French cookery, 169.
French domestic cookery, 157, 177.
French family cook, 121.
Frugal housekeeper's companion, 141.
Frugal housewife, 122, 168.

Gastronomic regenerator, 176.
Gastronomy, 142.
General receipt-book, 170, 171.
Genteel house-keepers pastime, 44.
Gentleman's companion and tradesman's delight, 65.
Gentlewomans cabinet unlocked, 33.
Gentlewoman's companion, 36.
Good house-wife made a doctor, 43.
Good hous-wives treasurie, 9.
Good huswifes handmaide for the kitchin, 10.
Good huswifes jewell, 7.
Good huswives handmaid for cookerie, 11.
Guide to preferment, 130.
Guide to trade. The confectioner, 172.

Health's grand preservative, 43.
Healths improvement, 27.
Hermeticall banquet, 22.
Hints for the table, 171.
Home book, 163.
Honours of the table, 116.
Householders philosophie, 9.
Housekeeper's accompt-book, 147.
Housekeeper's domestic library, 138.

House-keepers guide, 50, 167.
Housekeeper's instructor, 133.
Housekeeper's ledger, 146.
Housekeeper's magazine and family economist, 156.
Housekeeper's oracle, 162.
House-keeper's pocket-book, 63, 115.
Housekeeper's valuable present, 126.
Housewifes companion, 36.
Housewife's guide, 165, 167, 170, 172.
Hygiasticon, 20.

Ice book, 174.
Imperial and royal cook, 136.
Instructions in household matters, 175.
Instructor, 74.
Italian confectioner, 149.

Jewish manual, 176.

Kidd's Instructions, 167.
Kidd's Practical hints, 167.
Kitchen physick, 38.
Klinike, 20.

Ladies best companion, 127.
Ladies cabinet enlarged and opened, 21.
Ladies cabinet opened, 21.
Ladies companion, 25, 87.
Ladies delight, 35, 104.
Ladies directory, 31.
Ladies library, 119.
Lady's assistant, 107.
Lady's companion, 70, 84.
Lady's complete guide, 117.
Lady's, housewife's, and cookmaid's assistant, 100.
Lincolnshire family jewel, 136.
Little olde booke of cookerie, 3.
London and country cook, 77.
London art of cookery, 114.
London complete art of cookery, 124.
London cook, 92.

Madam Johnson's present, 83.
Magazine of domestic economy, 169.

INDEX OF TITLES

Miscellania, 43.
Mrs. Mary Eales's receipts, 55.
Mrs. Rundle's Young housekeeper's pocket account book, 136.
Modern art of cookery improved, 95.
Modern cook, 63, 177.
Modern cookery, 149, 175.
Modern domestic cookery, 143.
Modern family receipt-book, 158.
Modern housewife, 180.
Modern method of regulating and forming a table, 80.
Modern receipt book, 149.
Modern system of domestic cookery, 161.
Monthly observations, 43.
Mysteryes of nature and art, 20.

Naturall and artificial directions, 13.
New and complete universal cook, 111.
New and easy method of cookery, 88.
New book of cookerie, 17.
New book of cookery, 109.
New curiosities in art and nature, 53.
New digester, 40.
New experienced English housekeeper, 123.
New family receipt-book, 137, 145.
New London and country cook, 103.
New London cookery, 162.
New London family cook, 129.
New practice, 134.
New system of domestic cookery, 135.
New system of practical domestic economy, 166.
New system of vegetable cookery, 150.
New, universal, and complete confectioner, 110.
Newe boke of cokery, 3.

Olde mans dietarie, 8.

Pastry-cook's and confectioner's assistant, 172.
Pastry-cooks vade-mecum, 49.
Pearle of practice, 26.
Peptic precepts, 146.
Perfect cook, 28.
Perfect school of instructions, 42.
Philosophers banquet, 15.
Plain dealing poulterer, 39.
Practical economy, 149.
Practice of cookery, 120, 163.
Practice of modern cookery, 113.
Precious treasury of twenty rare secrets, 21.
Present for a servant-maid, 73.
Primitive cookery, 97.
Professed cook, 101.
Professed cookery, 91.
Proper newe booke of cokerye, 3.
Prudent housewife, 82.
Pythagorean diet of vegetables only, 76.

Queen-like closet, 35.
Queens closet opened, 26.
Queen's delight, 26.
Queen's royal cookery, 51.

Rare and excellent receipts, 40.
Receipts of pastry and cookery, 71.
Return to nature, 140.
Royal cookery, 52.
Royal Parisian pastry cook, 168.

School for good living, 142.
School of Salerne, 14.
Schoolemaster, 6.
Second collection. The general receipt-book, 171.
Second part of the good huswife's jewell, 8.
Secrete of Alexis, 3.
Servant's directory, 89.
Short treatise, 174.

Tabella cibaria, 148.
Thousand notable things, 12.
Town and country cook, 91.
Town and country cookery, 136.
Treasure of poore men, 2.

Treasurie of commodious conceites, 4.
Treasurie of hidden secrets, 5.
Treatise of cleanness in meats and drinks, 43.
Treatise of foods in general, 48.
True gentlewoman's delight, 22.
True preserver and restorer of health, 41.
True way of preserving and candying, 40.
Two bookes of cookerie and carving, 19.

Universal cook, 120.
Universal library, 181.

Valuable secrets concerning arts and trades, 108.
Vegetable cookery, 167.
Via recta ad vitam longam, 18.

Walker's new family receipt book, 170.
Way to get wealth, 43.
Way to health, 43.
Way to make all people rich, 43
Way to save wealth, 43.
Whole art of confectionary, 157
Whole art of curing, 177.
Whole body of cookery dissected, 30.
Whole duty of a woman, 46, 69.
Widdowes treasure, 11.
Wisdom's dictates, 43.

Young cook's guide, 169.
Young cooks monitor, 43.
Young ladies' guide, 108.
Young ladies' school of arts, 96.
Young lady's companion, 64.
Young woman's companion, 83, 140.

www.ingramcontent.com/pod-product-compliance
Lightning Source LLC
Chambersburg PA
CBHW021949290426
44108CB00012B/994